THE FASHION CLASSICS

THE FASHION CLASSICS

Copyright © Clare Faulkner, 2026

All illustrations © Clare Faulkner

All rights reserved.

No part of this book may be reproduced by any means, nor transmitted, nor translated into a machine language, without the written permission of the publishers.

Clare Faulkner has asserted their right to be identified as the author of this work in accordance with sections 77 and 78 of the Copyright, Designs and Patents Act 1988.

Condition of Sale
This book is sold subject to the condition that it shall not, by way of trade or otherwise, be lent, resold, hired out or otherwise circulated in any form of binding or cover other than that in which it is published and without a similar condition including this condition being imposed on the subsequent purchaser.

An Hachette UK Company
www.hachette.co.uk

Summersdale Publishers
Part of Octopus Publishing Group Limited
Carmelite House
50 Victoria Embankment
LONDON
EC4Y 0DZ
UK

This FSC® label means that materials and other controlled sources used for the product have been responsibly sourced

www.summersdale.com

The authorized representative in the EEA is Hachette Ireland, 8 Castlecourt Centre, Dublin 15, D15 XTP3, Ireland (email: info@hbgi.ie)

Printed and bound in China

ISBN: 978-1-83799-813-5
eISBN: 978-1-83799-814-2

Substantial discounts on bulk quantities of Summersdale books are available to corporations, professional associations and other organizations. For details contact general enquiries: telephone: +44 (0) 1243 771107 or email: enquiries@summersdale.com.

This book is unofficial and has not been authorized, licensed or endorsed by the brands mentioned within – it is written for fans by fans of fashion. Every effort has been made to ensure that all information is correct. Should there be any errors, we apologize and shall be pleased to make the appropriate amendments in any future editions.

THE FASHION CLASSICS

100 ICONIC & TIMELESS DESIGNS

Clare Faulkner

Contents

1	**Max Mara**, 101801 Camel Coat	26	**Gucci**, Jersey Dress
2	**Diane von Fürstenberg**, Wrap Dress	27	**Pierre Cardin**, Bubble Dress
3	**Mary Quant**, Mary Jane Shoe	28	**Courrèges**, Trouser Suit
4	**Hermès**, Birkin Bag	29	**Yves Saint Laurent**, Pea Coat
5	**Levi's**, 501 Jeans	30	**Gucci**, Jackie Bag
6	**Calvin Klein**, Slip Dress	31	**Ralph Lauren**, Suit
7	**Nike**, Air Force 1 Shoe	32	**John Galliano**, Bias-Cut Dress
8	**Katharine Hamnett**, Slogan T-Shirt	33	**Dr. Martens**, 1460 Boot
9	**Burberry**, Trench Coat	34	**Yves Saint Laurent**, Le Smoking Suit
10	**Fendi**, Baguette Handbag	35	**Dior**, Lady Dior Bag
11	**Chanel**, Twinset	36	**Maison Martin Margiela**, Tabi Boot
12	**Balenciaga**, Sack Dress	37	**Balenciaga**, Baby Doll Dress
13	**Converse**, Chuck Taylor All Star Shoe	38	**Vivienne Westwood**, Corset
14	**Donna Karan**, Bodysuit	39	**Pucci**, Silk Jersey Dress
15	**Jean Paul Gaultier**, Bomber Jacket	40	**Jean Muir**, Jersey Dress
16	**Ralph Lauren**, Polo Shirt	41	**OMO Norma Kamali**, Sleeping Bag Coat
17	**Mary Quant**, Minidress	42	**Balenciaga**, City Bag
18	**Giorgio Armani**, Blazer	43	**Stephen Burrows**, Colour Block Dress
19	**Issey Miyake**, Pleats Please Dress	44	**Jean Paul Gaultier**, Corset Dress
20	**Halston**, Shirt Dress	45	**Paco Rabanne**, Discs Dress
21	**Biba**, Evening Dress	46	**Dior**, Bar Suit
22	**Saint James**, Breton Top	47	**Digby Morton**, Aran Jumper Dress
23	**Valentino Garavani**, Rockstud Pump	48	**Alexander McQueen**, Tartan Dress
24	**Salvatore Ferragamo**, Wedge Shoe	49	**Sonja de Lennart**, Capri Pants
25	**Chanel**, Tweed Jacket	50	**Gucci**, Horsebit Loafer

> "Hitch your wagon to the steady stars that continue to shine on year after year."
> *Edith Head*

51	**Burberry**, Cashmere Scarf	76	**Norman Norell**, Mermaid Dress
52	**Laulhère**, Beret	77	**Adidas**, Samba Trainer
53	**Louis Vuitton**, Speedy Bag	78	**Hermès**, Kelly Bag
54	**Chanel**, Little Black Dress	79	**Vivienne Westwood**, Suit
55	**Adidas**, Tracksuit	80	**Jacques Fath**, Cocktail Dress
56	**Fiorucci**, Stretch Jeans	81	**Birkenstock**, Arizona Sandal
57	**Barbour**, Beaufort Waxed Jacket	82	**Hervé Léger**, Bandage Dress
58	**Chanel**, Slingback	83	**Alexander McQueen**, Knuckle Clutch
59	**Marc Jacobs**, Stam Bag	84	**Dior**, Aiguille Heel
60	**Jimmy Choo**, Lance Sandal	85	**Hermès**, Carré Scarf
61	**Roland Mouret**, Galaxy Dress	86	**Yohji Yamamoto**, White Shirt
62	**Prada**, Vela Backpack	87	**Levi's**, Trucker Jacket
63	**Dior**, Pencil Skirt	88	**Champion**, Hoodie
64	**Yves Saint Laurent**, Safari Jacket	89	**Manolo Blahnik**, Maysale Mule
65	**Ray-Ban**, Wayfarer Sunglasses	90	**Dior**, Trapeze Dress
66	**Yves Saint Laurent**, Jumpsuit	91	**UGG**, Classic Mini Boot
67	**Givenchy**, Sheath Dress	92	**Dior**, Turtleneck Sweater
68	**Balenciaga**, Cocoon Coat	93	**Prada**, Galleria Handbag
69	**New Era**, 59FIFTY Cap	94	**Gianni Versace**, Oroton Dress
70	**Chanel**, 2.55 Handbag	95	**Alaïa**, Zip Dress
71	**Jacques Esterel**, Bardot Top	96	**Lucchese**, Cowboy Boot
72	**Jean Barthet**, Wide-Brimmed Hat	97	**Gucci**, Silk Shirt
73	**Saint Laurent**, Biker Jacket	98	**Valentino**, Fiesta Dress
74	**Courrèges**, Go-Go Boot	99	**Hermès**, Oran Sandal
75	**Claire McCardell**, Popover Dress	100	**Salvatore Ferragamo**, Vara Ballet Flat

Introduction

"The message I would like to send is to buy less but choose well."
Vivienne Westwood

Welcome to the heady world of fashion, where anything goes but the enduring classics still rule – and with good reason. To earn a place in *The Fashion Classics*, a design must be iconic, influential and timeless, but, most importantly, it must be wearable.

Some of the items on these pages are recognized the world over, from the famous Hermès Kelly bag to legendary Levi's 501 jeans, while others – such as the Donna Karan adaptable bodysuit and Sonja de Lennart flattering Capri pants – have quietly changed what women wear. Some heritage items have a long history: the Burberry trench coat and Saint James Breton top, for example, have their roots in tradition, while others, such as Prada's Galleria handbag, have entered the fashion hall of fame in more recent years and rapidly gained classic status.

While there is only space for 100 fashion items on these pages, many more exceptional designs and designers exist beyond this list. Designers are influenced by each other and the people they design for, so in some cases the specific item featured here represents a wider adoption of a style, such as the Saint Laurent biker jacket, which brought street style to the catwalk with a nod to Schott Bros' pioneering jacket of 1928. The items here do not appear in a specific order; rather they are mixed up to reflect the ebb and flow of styles through the decades – great fashion is timeless, after all!

While some of the items will be out of reach for many of us, if your budget doesn't stretch to Chanel or Burberry, take note from master couturier Christian Dior who advised "simplicity, good taste and grooming are the three fundamentals of good dressing and these do not cost money." Finding your own classics – those beautifully crafted items that will last season after season – without blowing the budget, is the key to developing and defining your own unique style. Investing in well-made pieces designed to last and transcend trends, while embracing preloved and vintage, is ultimately better for our pockets and the world.

The purpose of this book is to celebrate those iconic items that have changed what we wear, rather than interrogate the environmental or ethical credentials of a piece, but it's important to remember that as consumers we have the power to choose. Some designers and brands are leading the way by experimenting with innovative materials and production methods, but there is a long way to go before fashion becomes sustainable, and we *can* vote with our purses. Spending more on less and choosing those items that boost your confidence and transform your wardrobe for the long term could be a great place to start.

I hope you enjoy the fascinating and surprising stories of these iconic examples from modern fashion history, and find inspiration for building a wardrobe of fashion classics that reflect your *own* inimitable style.

1

Max Mara
101801 Camel Coat

"A Max Mara coat comes from a search for balance between fabric, shape, colour and manufacturing to reach perfection."
Anne-Marie Beretta

In a ground-breaking move, Achille Maramotti, founder of Italian company Max Mara, reconceived the traditional men's camel coat for women in the 1950s, but it was designer Anne-Marie Beretta who created the iconic 101801 version in 1981. Known for her sculptural approach to clothing design, Beretta's take on the coat has become the company's most famous and cherished model. The long, oversized coat is known for its chic cut, kimono-style sleeves, exceptional quality and longevity – an investment that will surely never go out of fashion.

2

Diane von Fürstenberg Wrap Dress

"The whole thing about that dress is real – it suits everybody."
Sarah Jessica Parker

Diane von Fürstenberg's iconic wrap dress launched in the early 1970s and became an immediate classic. Taking inspiration from ballerinas' wrap tops and sportswear, the clingy dresses in bold prints were loved for their comfort, practicality and immensely flattering fit. The wrap dress was appropriate for work but could also be worn in the evening. They were hugely sought-after in the 1970s and are still treasured around the world today – with admirers including Michelle Obama and Madonna – for their versatility and effortless style.

3

Mary Quant
Mary Jane Shoe

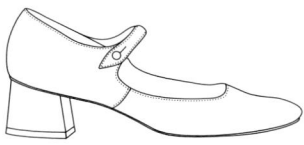

"I had idolized a little girl we knew who took tap-dancing lessons and wore… black patent ankle strap shoes."
Mary Quant

Originally the shoes of little girls and boys, the comfortable and cute Mary Jane has enjoyed plenty of time in the fashion spotlight. In the 1960s, Mary Quant chose black tap shoes for Twiggy, and helped popularize Mary Janes throughout the decade, along with other designers and it-girls. These Mary Quant shoes from the mid-1960s are still wearable classics today. Worn by Courtney Love in the 1990s, and embraced by Manolo Blahnik (in their Campari Mary Janes) and Maison Margiela (in their Tabi Mary Janes), the Mary Jane continues to be reinvented and reimagined by designers and style icons.

4

Hermès
Birkin Bag

"I said: 'The day Hermès makes one with pockets I will have that.'"
Jane Birkin

The it-bag that debuted in 1984 was created for style icon Jane Birkin after a chance encounter with Jean-Louis Dumas of Hermès on a flight from Paris to London. Birkin and Dumas dreamed up the spacious and flexible holdall together after Birkin bemoaned the lack of pockets and space in handbags. The much sought-after Birkin features two rolled handles, a flap top, lock closure and four *clou* "feet". Beloved by stars and the fashion pack alike – from Kate Moss to Winnie Harlow – the bag is a lasting investment that is made to be used.

5 Levi's 501 Jeans

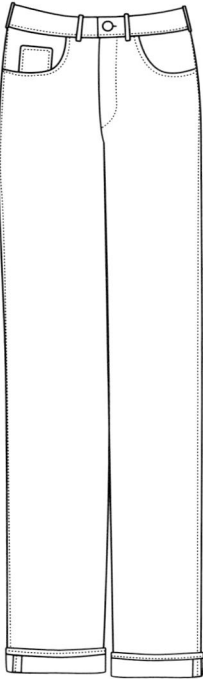

"There are jeans – baggy, skinny, flared, what-have-you, that go in and out of style – and then there's the 501s, the one true jean."
British Vogue

A classic in the truest sense of the word, the legendary 501 jeans have been around for more than 150 years and their iconic features, from the distinctive rivets to the button fly, are known the world over. In the 1950s the denim trousers began to transcend their workwear origins, and when screen stars such as Marilyn Monroe were seen wearing them their popularity rapidly grew beyond cult status. Seemingly adopted by every youth subculture going, 501s are the blank canvas every wardrobe needs. Designed for durability, comfort and the perfect fit, like a fine wine, these jeans only get better with age. 501s are the ultimate fashion staple, loved for their versatility, craftsmanship and effortless style.

6

Calvin Klein
Slip Dress

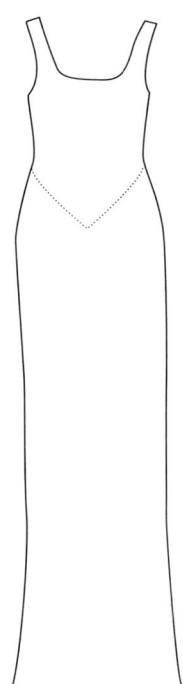

"Calvin's clothing seemed to be all about the sensation of touch."
Marc Jacobs

The 1990s were defined by the slip dress, and Calvin Klein's Spring/Summer 1994 show confirmed it had well and truly arrived. The slip dress exuded an effortless chic and the carefree suggestion of wearing underwear as outerwear gave the garment more than a whiff of rebellion. Calvin Klein became known for minimalist elegance and his slip dresses were easy to fling on, could be dressed up or down, and worn day or night. They were light, floaty, neutral in palette and perfect for the new waif aesthetic. The slip dress remains an essential part of the modern wardrobe and Veronica Leoni's recent debut collection at Calvin Klein included silky versions, with Kate Moss in attendance sporting one.

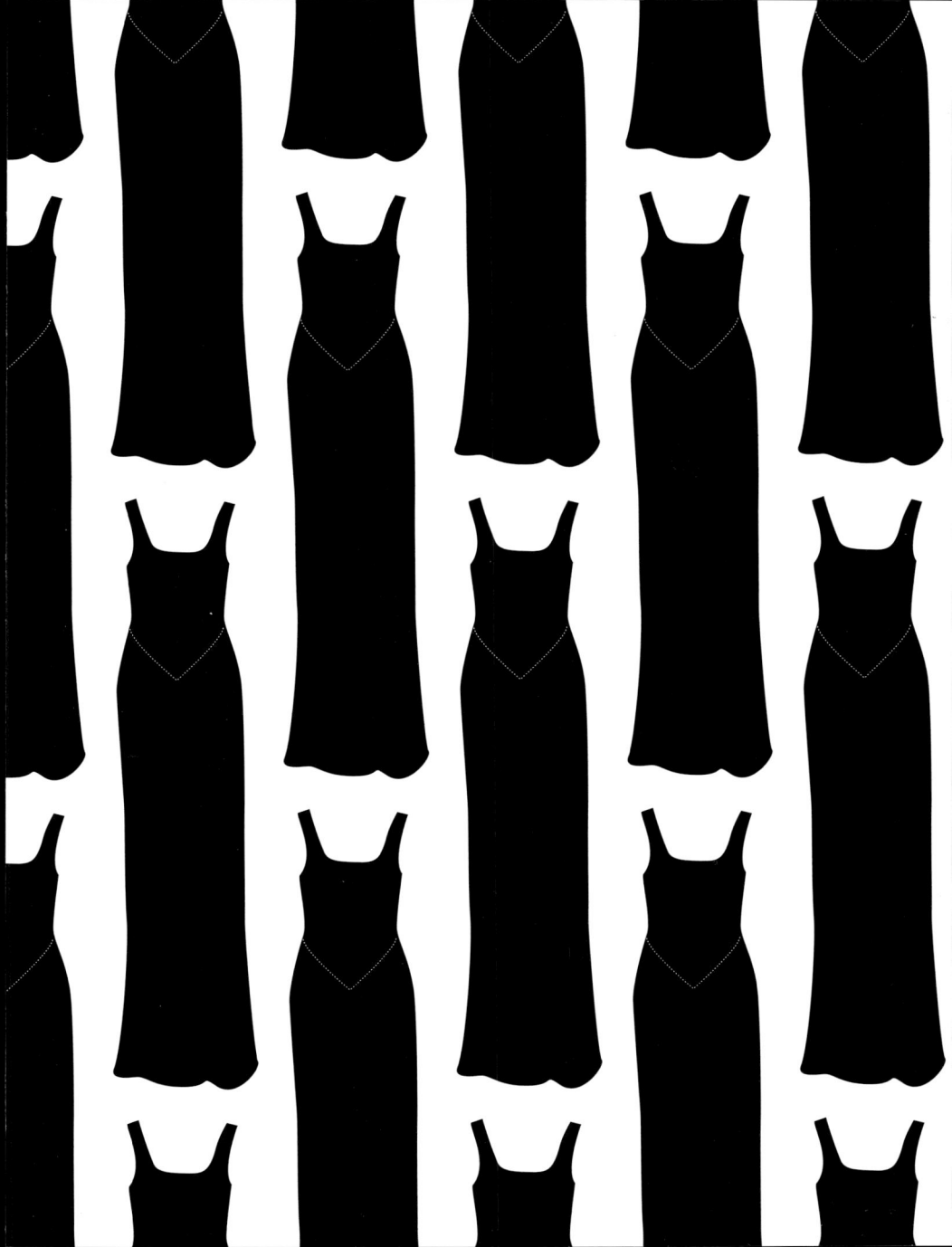

7

Nike
Air Force 1 Shoe

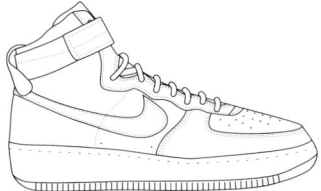

"I would pair them with everything."
Bella Hadid

Nike's bestselling shoe was released in 1982 and quickly became a cult classic. It was designed by Bruce Kilgore, and inspired by a Nike hiking boot to provide more support and stability for basketball players. The original white-and-grey high-top has been through countless reiterations, updates and collaborations since, but retains those important signature features. The classic and minimalist white-on-white is the unrivalled style leader; and celebrities can't get enough of them, with devotees including Lizzo and Kendall Jenner.

8

Katharine Hamnett
Slogan T-Shirt

"With those T-shirts, it was about putting ideas into people's heads."
Katharine Hamnett

Katharine Hamnett's memorable white T-shirts first appeared in 1983, debuting with her peace-seeking "Choose Life" design in large, bold black type. The slogan was inspired by Buddhism's principle to do no harm. Hamnett understood the power of the human canvas, and the T-shirt was quickly adopted by popstars including George Michael. Many challenging slogans swiftly followed, and Hamnett became known for her political activism and ceaseless battle for sustainability in fashion. However, she warns, "T-shirts and marches don't change anything unless they're followed up with political engagement."

Burberry
Trench Coat

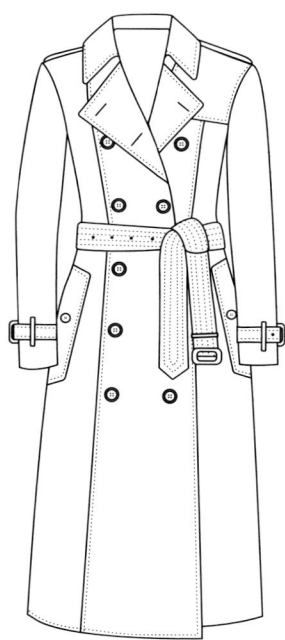

"Inherent in every Burberry garment is freedom."
Thomas Burberry

The Burberry trench coat was developed by Thomas Burberry for First World War officers and has been a steadfast wardrobe classic ever since. Using Burberry's innovative cotton gabardine fabric – the strands of which were individually waterproofed before weaving – the trench was breathable, weatherproof and light, and was hand-finished by specialist tailors. The coat was first lined with the distinctive Burberry check in the 1920s, and Hollywood stars from Sophia Loren to Meryl Streep soon cemented its status as a timeless icon. The versatility and craftsmanship of this coat makes it an essential investment piece and worthy of its revered status.

10

Fendi
Baguette Handbag

"Sentimental, lady, modern – and surprisingly timeless."
Sarah Jessica Parker

First created for the Italian luxury brand in 1997 by Silvia Venturini Fendi, the Baguette has become one of the world's most famous handbags. Observing that others were lacking originality, Venturini Fendi designed a petite and short-strapped handbag in "many decorated versions" and the Baguette was born. It quickly took off and the variety of colours and designs available – often limited editions – created a frenzy. The status of the handbag was underlined when Carrie Bradshaw, sporting a purple-sequinned version in *Sex and the City*, corrected her bag-snatching mugger: "It's a Baguette."

11

Chanel
Twinset

"Chanel is master of her art, and her art resides in jersey."
British Vogue

Gabrielle "Coco" Chanel is credited with one of the earliest examples of the twinset, along with heritage brand Pringle, and popularized jersey versions of the two-piece in the 1920s. The twinset soared in popularity in the 1940s and 50s, with Hollywood stars including Grace Kelly and Marilyn Monroe modelling figure-enhancing sweaters with matching cardigans. A pink cashmere Pringle twinset even made the cover of *Vogue* in 1955. Karl Lagerfeld frequently referenced Coco Chanel's iconic pieces during his tenure and the twinset illustrated here from the Autumn/Winter 1994 collection is an elegant reinvention of Chanel's classic.

12 Balenciaga
Sack Dress

"In a Balenciaga, you were the only woman in the room."
Diana Vreeland

Master couturier Cristóbal Balenciaga was known for experimenting with the silhouette. Against the backdrop of the 1950s hourglass figure, in 1957 he introduced the "sack" dress, a loose-fitting garment that eliminated the waist. It was not an immediate success and received criticism from clients and the press, but the innovative style eventually became a highly influential shape. This fluid and unique style allowed women a new freedom of movement and has an understated sophistication that makes it a true classic piece.

13

Converse Chuck Taylor All Star Shoe

"It's just something in the design that's really universal."
M.I.A.

First launched as All Stars in 1917, with the Chuck Taylor signature following in the 1930s, "Chucks" are iconic and arguably the most famous shoes in the world. Embraced by rock stars, models and Hollywood stars through this century and the last, the high-top sneakers are failsafe staples for every wardrobe. Renowned for their distinctive features, including the famous ankle patch, contrasting stripes and durable canvas upper, the shoes are unmistakeable. Guaranteed to bring an effortless cool to any outfit, they simply get better the more you wear them.

14

Donna Karan
Bodysuit

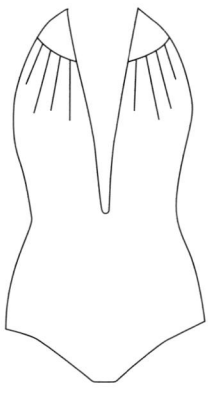

"A woman is her body, her sensuality, and her tailoredness, so I combined them together."
Donna Karan

Donna Karan put the "body" at the heart of her "Seven Easy Pieces" collection in 1985 and the revolutionary idea quickly became extremely influential. Inspiration came from the bodysuit Karan wore for yoga, and she set out to design a wardrobe for the working woman that was practical, comfortable and sensual. The bodysuits had different necklines and sleeves, and could be combined with additional "easy pieces" including a skirt, jacket, trousers, dress and sweater. This capsule wardrobe could take you through a day at the office and into the evening with ease.

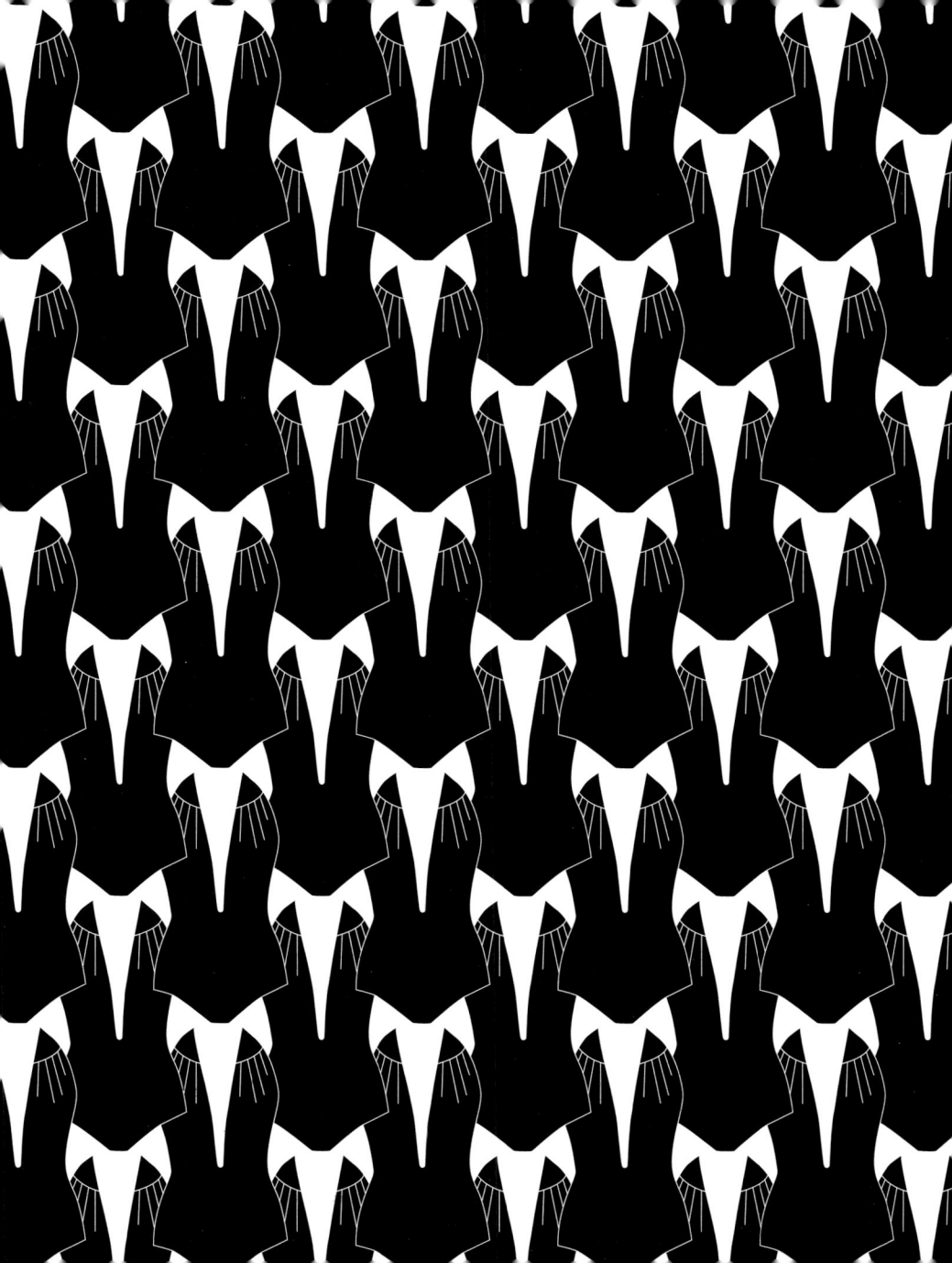

15
Jean Paul Gaultier
Bomber Jacket

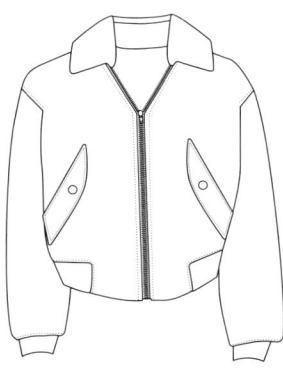

"The only designer clever enough to successfully re-invent one of the 1980s' most visible garments – the MA-1 flying jacket."
The Face

The now-iconic MA-1 flying jacket was created in 1948 by Dobbs Industries, now Alpha Industries, and introduced to the US military in 1949. In the following decades, it was adopted by various subcultures and, during the late 1980s, Jean Paul Gaultier introduced the bomber jacket to high fashion. Katharine Hamnett also helped popularize the bomber jacket around the same time with her own version, inspired by street style. Gaultier played with the basic silhouette by introducing cropped styles for women through his "Junior" line, and the jacket became a signature style for the designer. Both the genuine military pieces and the countless reinterpretations remain versatile wardrobe staples.

16 Ralph Lauren Polo Shirt

"It was never about a shirt, but a way of living."
Ralph Lauren

Introduced in 1972 for the "Polo" line, the Ralph Lauren polo shirt enjoyed immediate success and has endured to become an everlasting, all-American classic. Famous for its sharp collar, contrasting logo and bold colours, the polo shirt is a versatile component of any contemporary wardrobe. From supermodels to politicians, sports and Hollywood stars, it has been worn by everyone and continues to be beloved by people from all walks of life. Dress it up or down to suit the mood.

17 Mary Quant Minidress

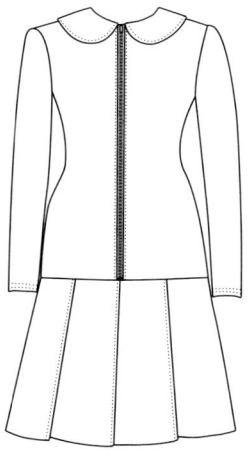

"I wanted girls to move, jump, be alive!"
Mary Quant

Quant revolutionized women's fashion in many ways, but her wool-jersey fabric minidresses are one of her most influential innovations. Quant wanted fashion to allow women to live their busy lives without restriction, and designed many minidresses in this comfortable and practical fabric in an array of styles and bold colours. This "skater"-style jersey dress from 1967 is a striking example of her ground-breaking but beautifully simple designs that are still wearable classics today.

18 Giorgio Armani
Blazer

"I set to work on women's jackets and created styles with a simple and soft shape... both powerful and feminine."
Giorgio Armani

Giorgio Armani brought his understated tailoring to women's suits in the late 1970s and became a forerunner in the introduction of relaxed work styles for women. Style icon Diane Keaton famously wore a casual Giorgio Armani jacket over a maxi skirt to accept her Best Actress award for *Annie Hall* in 1978, with Armani observing, "You can see how Diane makes a tailored jacket – in a style normally associated with a man's suit – look thoroughly modern and individual."

19

Issey Miyake
Pleats Please Dress

> **"Pleats Please is what I consider my most valuable contribution to 'design'."**
> *Issey Miyake*

Issey Miyake pioneered an innovative new technique in the late 1980s using a high-quality polyester that allowed garments to be exquisitely and permanently pleated. Extraordinarily, the clothes could be washed and worn and would still retain their delicate pleats. In 1993, Miyake launched the "Pleats Please Issey Miyake" line that would become a lasting success and a fashion editor's firm favourite. The crease-free style that adds sophistication to dresses, trousers and tops is an easily recognizable design feature and a valuable addition to any wardrobe.

20 Halston Shirt Dress

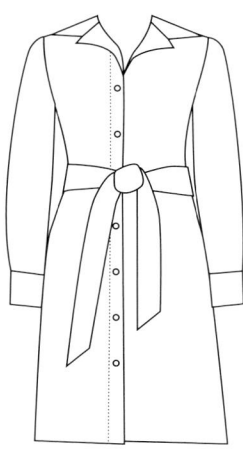

> *"I always wanted to change everything in clothing, to make it a little more simple, a little more American."*
>
> Roy Halston Frowick

Halston reignited an appetite for the "shirtwaist" dress in 1972 with a sophisticated design made in "Ultrasuede", a lightweight fabric with the velvety feel of suede. The dress became hugely popular, was widely copied and Halston became forever associated with the American design classic. Halston's shirt dress was constructed much like a man's shirt, but with tighter sleeves, an understated A-line shape and a co-ordinating belt that allowed for versatile individual styling. A-list devotees of Halston's minimalist designs included Liza Minnelli, Elizabeth Taylor and Bianca Jagger.

21

Biba
Evening Dress

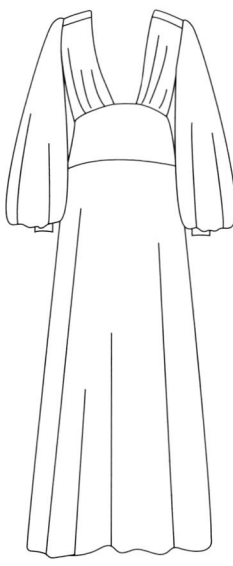

> *"It isn't just selling dresses, it's a whole way of life."*
> Barbara Hulanicki

Barbara Hulanicki and her husband Stephen Fitz-Simon opened the legendary Big Biba lifestyle store on Kensington High Street in 1973, the year they created the stylish maxi dress illustrated here. Visionary designer Hulanicki and Fitz-Simon had started Biba in the 1960s, offering exquisitely designed but affordable fashion for young women. Hulanicki's designs were inspired by the decadence of past eras including Art Deco and Art Nouveau. This luxurious viscose-jersey dress, with voluminous sleeves gathered at the cuffs and a plunging neckline, beautifully encapsulates the sophisticated glamour of Biba.

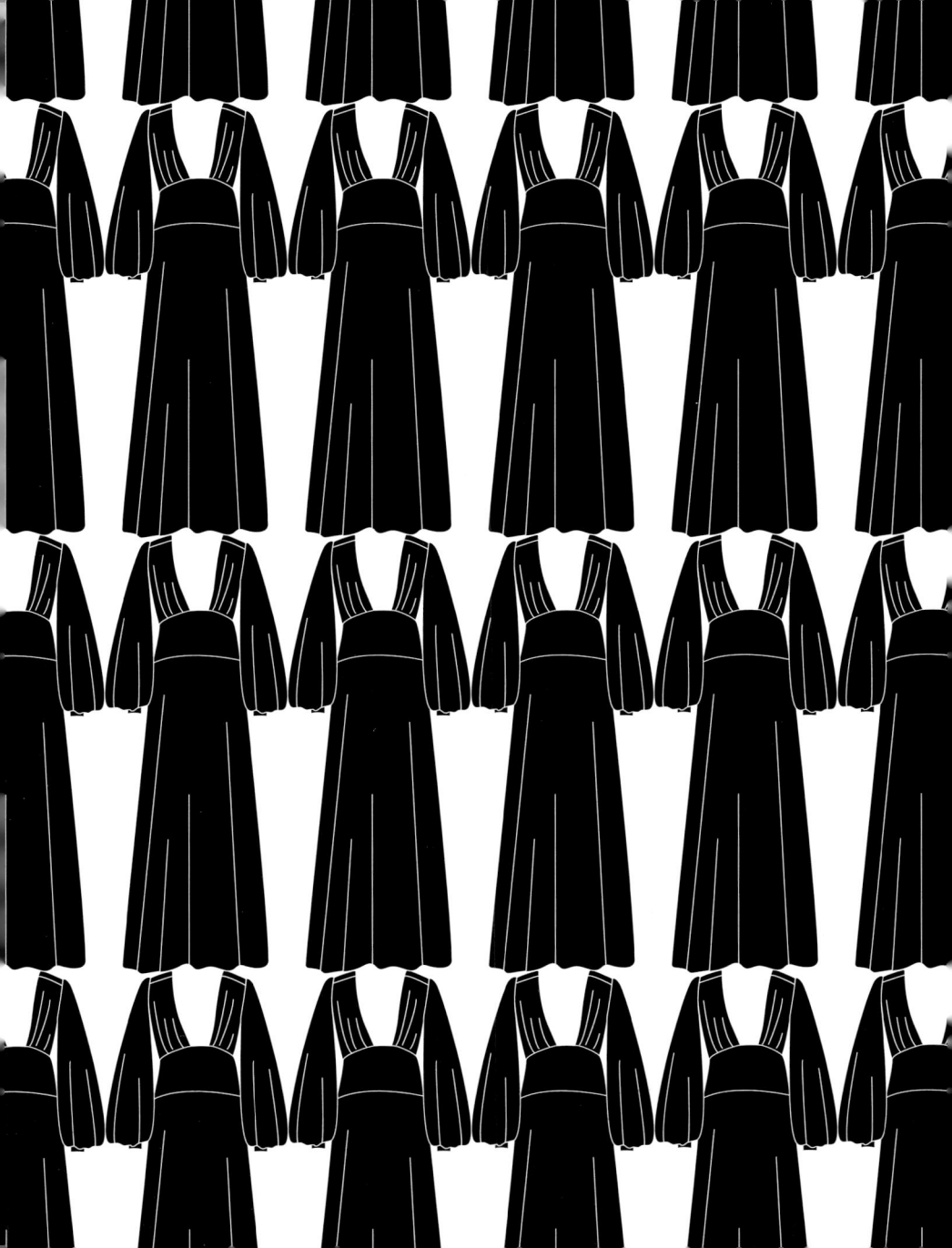

22

Saint James
Breton Top

"The OG of Breton tops."
Elle UK

Originally worn by fishermen, the classic horizontally striped *marinière* was adopted by the French navy in 1858. In the twentieth century it became a unisex wardrobe staple in France, and its classic status grew as a catalogue of icons including Coco Chanel, Brigitte Bardot, Jean Seberg and Audrey Hepburn popularized the style. Saint James' illustrious history along with pure craftsmanship makes its Breton the go-to for those looking for a true classic.

23
Valentino Garavani
Rockstud Pump

"When you see a Rockstud, it's a punk shoe, it's a bourgeois shoe, so it's a new balance between different cultures."
Pierpaolo Piccioli

Valentino co-creative directors Maria Grazia Chiuri and Pierpaolo Piccioli debuted these iconic studded stilettos in the Autumn/Winter 2010 collection – and they quickly became a symbol of rebellious chic. Referencing both the punk movement and architectural detail from Rome, the pyramidal-shaped studs give the shoes a covetable edginess. The sought-after Rockstuds have been designed in many iterations since and are bestsellers for the fashion house, season after season. They are perennial favourites with the A-list crowd, from Emma Stone to Gigi Hadid.

24

Salvatore Ferragamo Wedge Shoe

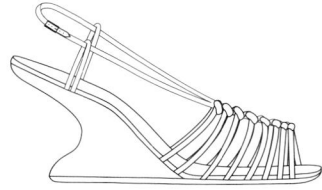

> **"We can all walk happily and be well shod, daintily shod, beautifully shod."**
> *Salvatore Ferragamo*

Ferragamo was famous for his innovative experimentation with shape and materials in his groundbreaking shoe designs. Faced with a lack of steel in the 1930s, he looked to the wedge shapes of bathing shoes and beachwear, drawing inspiration from these to devise and patent the cork wedge. The wedge became a hugely popular style and Ferragamo went on to develop the wooden F-heel with an elegantly curved back. Whether cork, wood or straw, the wedge has endured as an iconic shape through the decades and remains a comfortable alternative to heels.

25
Chanel
Tweed Jacket

"Some things never go out of fashion: jeans, the white shirt, and the Chanel jacket."
Karl Lagerfeld

First designed by Coco Chanel in 1954, the classic Chanel tweed jacket is arguably as famous as its inventor. The short, collarless jacket allowed freedom of movement and had unmistakeable features, such as its four pockets and braid trim. With meticulous attention to detail, including a chain in the lining to ensure it hung perfectly, the design became a classic. The ultimate symbol of relaxed luxury, it took the world by storm in the 1950s. The jacket has remained a truly elegant and adaptable piece through the decades, with Karl Lagerfeld continually reinventing the jacket at Chanel and keeping it at the forefront of the brand.

26 Gucci
Jersey Dress

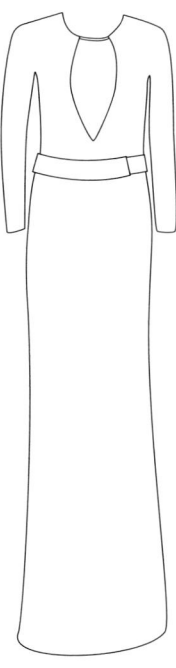

"I brought back a certain sexual glamour."
Tom Ford

Tom Ford's floor-length white column jersey dresses, with sensual cut-outs, keyholes and luxurious brass belts and details, brought decadent and classical style to Gucci's Autumn/Winter 1996 collection. *Vogue* declared the collection the "fashion equivalent of a one-night stand at Studio 54". Ford effortlessly combined the wild opulence of his youth at the New York club with a timeless, minimal elegance, and Gucci's status as a sophisticated luxury brand grew exponentially with his arrival as creative director in 1994.

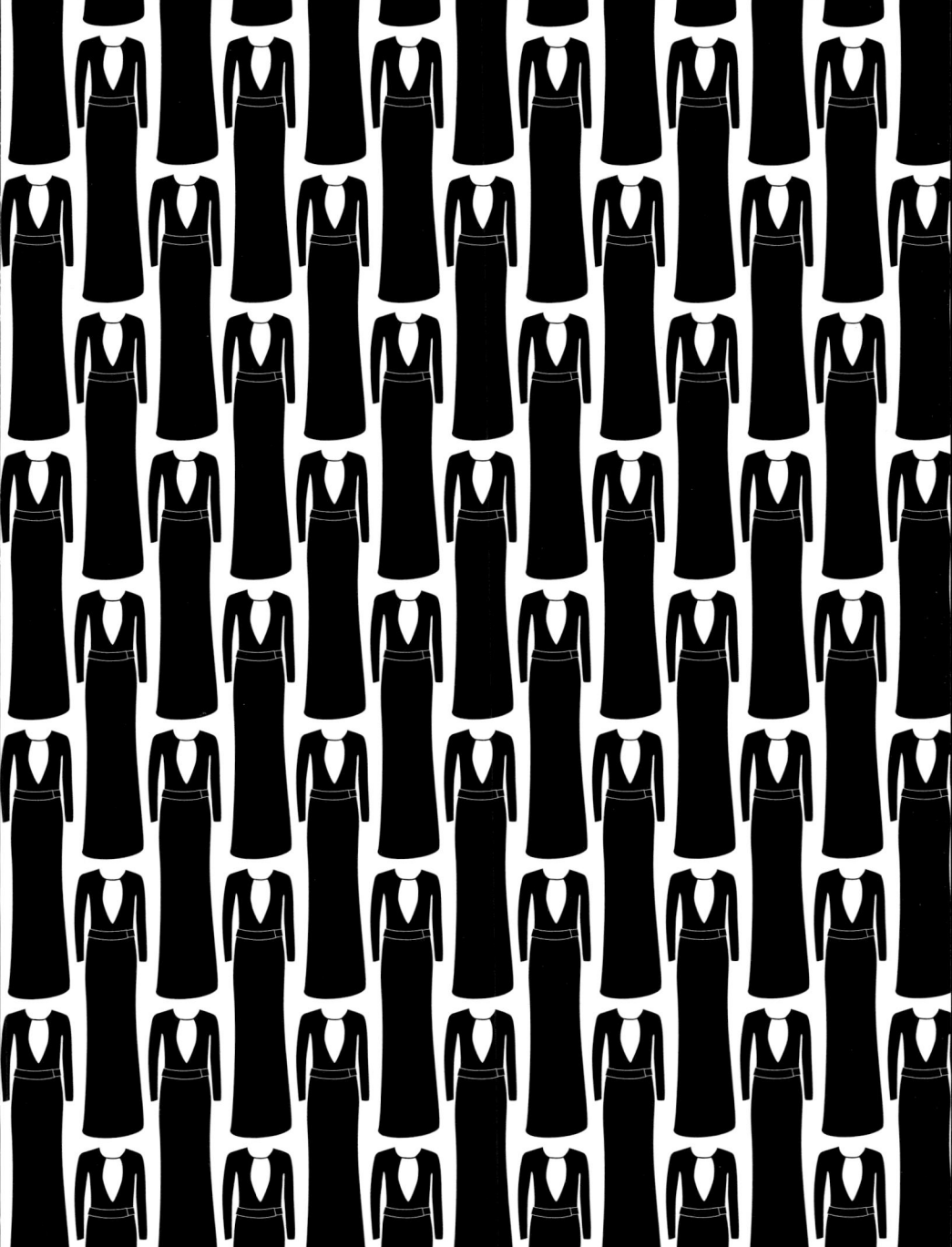

27

Pierre Cardin
Bubble Dress

> **"The clothes that I prefer are those I invent for a life that doesn't exist yet – the world of tomorrow."**
> *Pierre Cardin*

Pierre Cardin designed an innovative new shape for women in 1954 with the launch of his pioneering bubble dress. This sculptural layered dress flared from below the waist and gathered at the hem to create a radical new "bubble" shape. The dress was extremely successful internationally and the bubble hem remains a modern look in contemporary fashion. Pushing the boundaries of a woman's silhouette would become a frequent feature of Cardin's work.

28 Courrèges
Trouser Suit

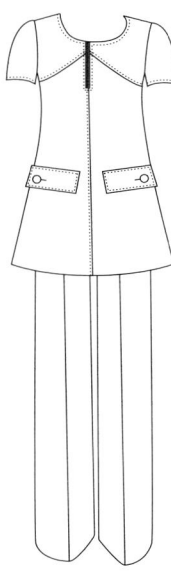

"There are occasions where pants are the thing to wear. They are more elegant on those occasions than any dress."
André Courrèges

André Courrèges was one of the first designers to introduce fitted, formal trousers for women, a radical concept in the 1960s. His pantsuits with narrow trousers were extremely influential on women's fashion, and this suit from the 1968 Courrèges ready-to-wear collection made them more accessible for the younger generation. Courrèges believed women's clothing should be practical and allow them to live their modern lives in freedom. Trousers were a logical but revolutionary progression in his futuristic vision for women.

29 Yves Saint Laurent
Pea Coat

**"It was based on a sailor's pea jacket…
It was a scandal."**
Yves Saint Laurent

The pea coat, worn with white trousers, opened the first collection under the Yves Saint Laurent name in 1962. Saint Laurent was frequently inspired by men's clothing and his pea coat design for women was seen as a radical step. But, nonetheless, the show was declared the "most beautiful collection since Chanel" by *Life*. The signature features of the double-breasted jacket – wide lapels, distinctive buttons, vertical pockets and often thick navy wool – have made the pea coat a chic classic for all.

30

Gucci
Jackie Bag

"The timeless design is a testament to the bag's enduring appeal."
Marie Claire UK

Debuting as the G1244 handbag in 1961, this iconic piece was later known as the "Jackie" after it came to be associated with style-setting Jacqueline Kennedy. The fashion icon reportedly had numerous versions of the distinctive bag, including a relaxed canvas version, and its success marked a cultural shift away from more traditionally shaped handbags. Gucci and the Jackie were widely adored during the 1970s and the bag has been redesigned through the decades by the fashion house without losing its unique soft crescent shape. The Jackie continues to be lauded for its versatility and relaxed elegance.

31

Ralph Lauren
Suit

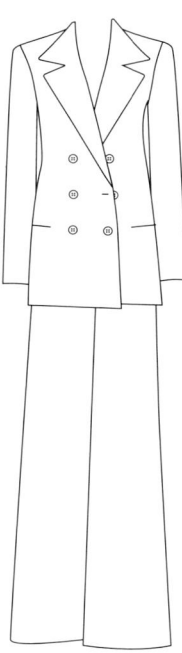

"He understands a woman's body in a man's style of suit… he uses durable fabrics that adhere to a body yet keep structure."
Diane Keaton

The 1980s saw the rise of the "power suit", reflecting the need for women in the workplace to assert their professional confidence. Designers including Giorgio Armani, Donna Karan and Ralph Lauren provided stylish no-nonsense suits for the work environment. Ralph Lauren understood how to cut a women's suit to flatter and empower, and the secret of the brand's success was in selling a lifestyle. The example illustrated here from the Ralph Lauren Spring/Summer 1989 collection is the epitome of understated style.

32

John Galliano
Bias-Cut Dress

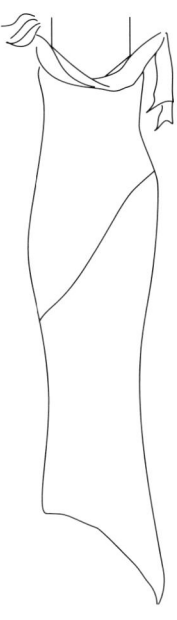

"The bias-cut slip dress really became a symbol of what women wore at night… and that was John."
Anna Wintour

John Galliano had already shown masterfully constructed slip dresses, inspired by French couturier Madeleine Vionnet's innovative bias-cut techniques. However, his Spring/Summer 1994 "Princess Lucretia" collection included dresses that would fast-track the deceptively simple slip dress to legendary status – and mark Galliano's arrival at the centre of fashion. The technique allowed the fabric to mould beautifully to the body, and Galliano's interpretation was both modern and fresh while referencing the glamour of the 1920s and 30s.

33

Dr. Martens
1460 Boot

"A model off-duty staple."
Vogue

Launched into the world on 1 April 1960 as a humble workwear boot, the 1460 has since become an undeniable classic. With distinctive features such as the thick air-cushioned sole, eight eyelets, signature stitching and black-and-yellow loop, the 1460 is an unmistakeable design icon. Seemingly adopted by every music tribe and subculture through the decades, Dr. Martens boots have remained culturally relevant and beloved the world over. Robust and enduring, the boots express the wearer's individualism and attitude in a way no other boot has been able to, and today's devotees include Dakota Johnson, Bella Hadid and Agyness Deyn.

34
Yves Saint Laurent
Le Smoking Suit

"For a woman, the tuxedo is an indispensable garment in which she will always feel in style."
Yves Saint Laurent

Saint Laurent debuted his legendary "Le Smoking" tuxedo for women at the Autumn/Winter haute couture show in 1966. Inspired by gentlemen's smoking jackets, the designer beautifully tailored the suit to fit and flatter the female body, with a thinner collar and narrowed waist. Initially, his clients were not ready for this bold statement, but intuitively Saint Laurent featured the design in his ready-to-wear line later that year and it was quickly embraced by younger women, if not by society at large. Bianca Jagger famously wore a white Le Smoking jacket to her wedding in 1971, and the decade saw the style take off and reach iconic status.

35

Dior
Lady Dior Bag

"A coveted treasure that will truly never go out of style."
Harper's Bazaar

The signature Dior handbag, originally known as "Chouchou", was renamed "Lady Dior" in 1995 in honour of Diana, Princess of Wales, after she adopted the bag before it became commercially available. The legendary square-shaped bag – first designed by Daniela Puppa during Gianfranco Ferré's tenure at Dior and exquisitely crafted in Italian workshops – features noteworthy "cannage" pattern quilting and hanging D, I, O and R charm letters. Since its first incarnation it has been redesigned and reimagined in different sizes, a variety of materials and many colours, and continues to be revered as a versatile accessory for both day and evening.

36

Maison Martin Margiela
Tabi Boot

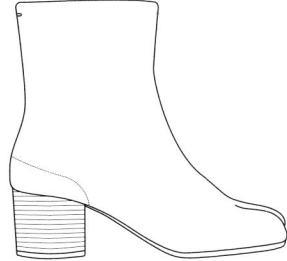

"You can imagine the stress when you want to create a shoe as never seen before."
Martin Margiela

In 1988, Martin Margiela debuted the Tabi boot and a cult classic for those in the know was born. The controversial split-toed shoe, which often inspires a strong reaction, was a designer take on the cotton "tabi" footwear that Margiela had seen on street workers in Tokyo. Margiela devised a heeled boot for the catwalk and the Tabi has since evolved into flats, trainers, stilettos and even the classic Mary Jane. John Galliano continued to reinvent the Tabi during his tenure and celebrities sporting the unique shoes include Cardi B, Sarah Jessica Parker and Chloë Sevigny.

37 Balenciaga Baby Doll Dress

"A woman has no need to be perfect or even beautiful to wear my dresses. The dress will do all that for her."
Cristóbal Balenciaga

In the late 1950s, Cristóbal Balenciaga introduced high fashion to his interpretation of the "baby doll" silhouette. Previously a shape associated with lingerie, Balenciaga's baby doll dresses also took inspiration from children's clothing styles. The girlish frocks with dropped waists, voluminous fabric, bow embellishments and drop sleeves were hugely influential. Balenciaga's first baby dolls often had an outer layer of lace revealing a fitted shape beneath. The hemline of the baby doll became ever shorter during the following decade and remains a popular shape in fashion today, with contemporary fans including Sabrina Carpenter.

38

Vivienne Westwood
Corset

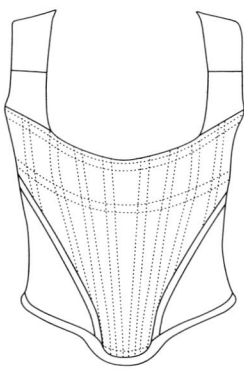

"When you explore the past, you enter the future."
Vivienne Westwood

Vivienne Westwood's iconic corsets first appeared in her Harris Tweed Autumn/Winter collection in 1987. Inspired by historical garments, Westwood's uniquely flattering and dramatic corset rethought underwear as outerwear, and rapidly became a signature look for the house. Although informed by eighteenth-century corsetry, Westwood used contemporary materials to modernize and innovate, such as high-strength zips and elastane. Widely appreciated for its masterful tailoring, the Vivienne Westwood corset remains both classic and striking.

39

Pucci
Silk Jersey Dress

"These fabrics are cut and put together to move with the person."
Emilio Pucci

Emilio Pucci, the "Prince of Prints", was known for his bold, multicoloured prints inspired by Florentine history. Most of the legendary prints began life on scarves before adorning dresses, tops and bikinis. One of Pucci's significant innovations was a silk jersey fabric, which was luxurious and sensuous, but also crease-resistant, making it immensely practical. A Pucci dress was a status symbol like no other in the 1960s – seen on Sophia Loren, Jacqueline Kennedy and Elizabeth Taylor – but the casual simplicity and unmistakeable prints make it a lasting classic.

40

Jean Muir
Jersey Dress

> "She has a real style you recognize and is unique… feminine but strong."
>
> *Jean Paul Gaultier*

The designer Jean Muir was revered for her exquisite dressmaking and timeless designs, often working in simple black and navy. This dress from 1973 was worn by Faye Dunaway in the pages of *Vogue*. Made from tactile jersey, with beautifully cut open handkerchief sleeves and a gathered waist, this sophisticated dress is both flattering and elegant. Early in Muir's career, *British Vogue* proclaimed she was "one of the new young names that are giving the sixties an accent all their own", and admirers of her work included Lauren Bacall and Diana Rigg.

41

OMO Norma Kamali Sleeping Bag Coat

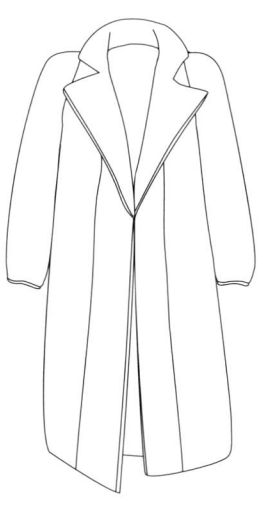

"I took my sleeping bag, and I cut a coat out of it."
Norma Kamali

Although down puffer coats had been around since the 1930s (an innovation by Eddie Bauer), Norma Kamali was the first to invent the ankle-length sleeping bag coat, in the early 1970s. Inspired by a cold camping trip, Kamali had the idea to add sleeves to a sleeping bag and the iconic coat was born. With a little help from the doormen modelling them at Studio 54 towards the end of the decade, the sleeping bag coat became a cult classic that has never gone out of style and has been spotted on icons including Rihanna and Lady Gaga.

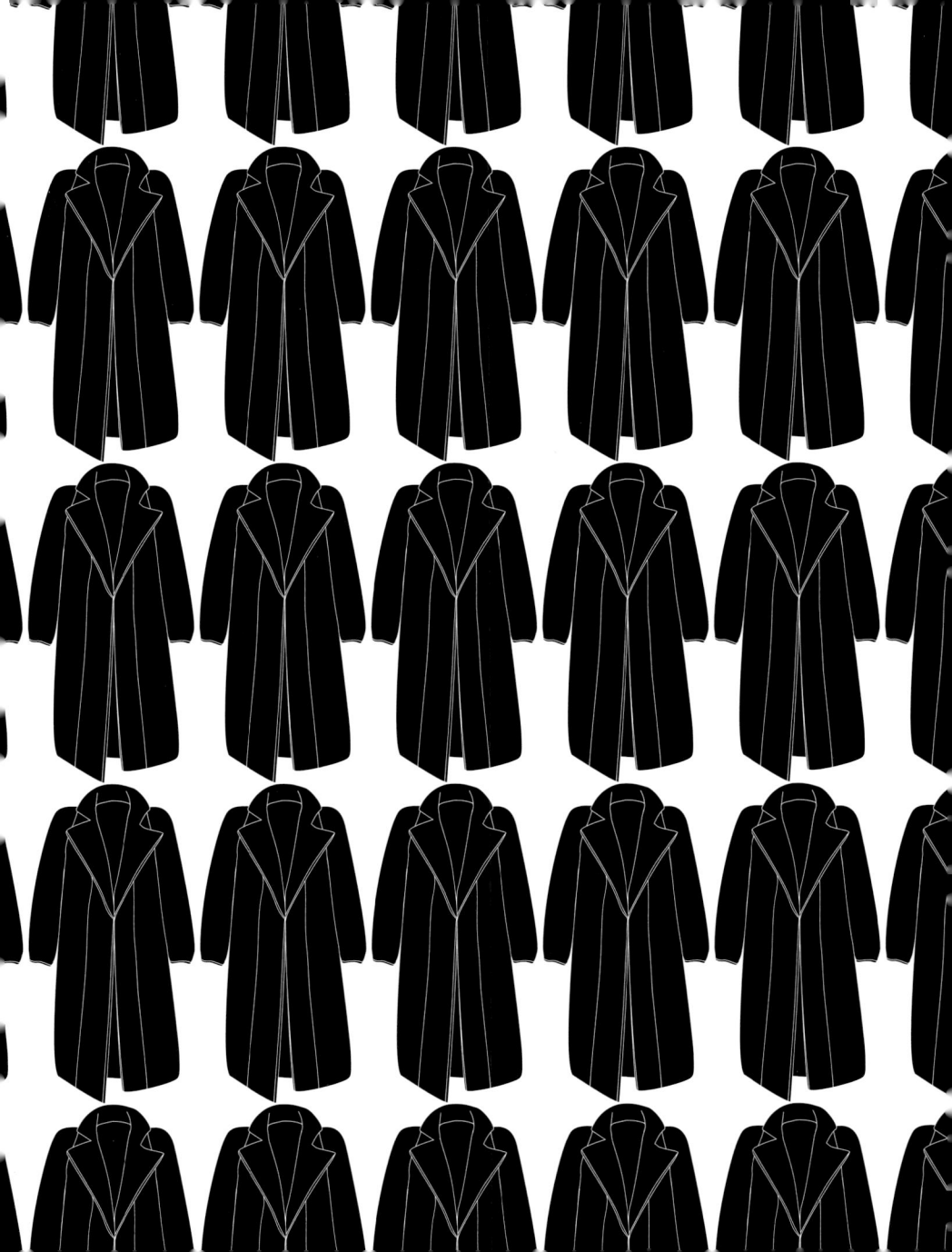

42

Balenciaga City Bag

"You could be a Balenciaga girl with that bag."
Nicolas Ghesquière

Balenciaga creative director Nicolas Ghesquière debuted the "motorcycle bag" in 2001 in its first incarnation as "Le Dix Motorcycle Lariat". Although the design wasn't initially well received by the house, following a nod of approval from Kate Moss it was renamed the "City" bag and, with its biker attitude, quickly became the it-bag to be seen with. The chic but nonchalant accessory has been through various iterations with different names since and is currently available as "Le City" in a range of sizes. It remains a must-have for many A-listers and is a relaxed and practical classic.

43

Stephen Burrows
Colour Block Dress

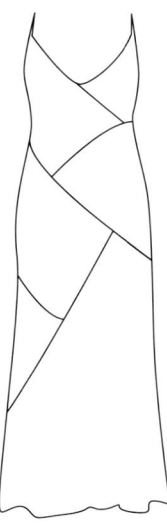

"Stephen created clothes that you could dance in."
Pat Cleveland

This jersey evening dress was featured in the legendary "Battle of Versailles" fashion show of 1973, which saw five American designers pitted against five based in Paris. Stephen Burrows' vibrant, flowing dresses, in innovative fabrics featuring striking and bold colour-block combinations, stole the show and were widely celebrated. Burrows was popular with style icons including Farrah Fawcett and Diana Ross, and his colour-block aesthetic continues to influence fashion. The playful, vivid designs are as fresh today as they were in the 1970s.

44

Jean Paul Gaultier
Corset Dress

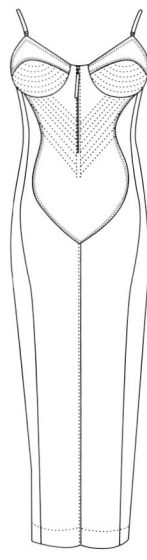

*"My raw material isn't fabric…
it's human beings."*
Jean Paul Gaultier

Jean Paul Gaultier's fascination with corsets began in childhood with his grandmother's extensive collection. In the 1980s, Gaultier helped to bring undergarments to the forefront of fashion and was most famous for his exaggerated cone bra. The legendary corseted body suit worn by Madonna on her Blond Ambition tour in 1990 echoes this less extreme corset dress from 1987. The beautifully constructed corset became a signature look for Jean Paul Gaultier and reclaimed the symbol of restriction for feminist sexuality.

45

Paco Rabanne
Discs Dress

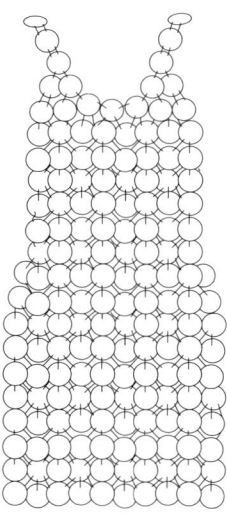

"The only new frontier left in fashion is the finding of new materials."
Paco Rabanne

Paco Rabanne's debut collection in 1966 was titled "Manifesto: 12 Unwearable Dresses in Contemporary Materials" – but his scandalous minidress turned out to be eminently wearable, albeit not entirely comfortable. Daringly see-through, the futuristic chain-mail dress was constructed from reflective plastic discs and metal links. It was innovative and experimental but ultimately proved to be an iconic fashion piece that continues to be relevant today. Audrey Hepburn famously wore a version in the film *Two for the Road*, elegantly proving even all-out bling can be classic and timeless.

46

Dior
Bar Suit

"The New Look became symbolic of youth and the future."
Christian Dior

In 1947, Christian Dior debuted the "Corolle" line, a revolutionary collection including the legendary Bar suit. An ivory jacket, with an hourglass waist and padding at the hips to emphasize the shapely curves, contrasted dramatically with a full, pleated woollen black skirt using a copious amount of fabric for the time. The elegant and simple shape was a huge success and was swiftly labelled the "New Look" by the press. The Bar jacket became a staple for the house and has been continually reimagined ever since by Dior creative directors including John Galliano.

47

Digby Morton
Aran Jumper Dress

"The ultimate sweater dress."
Vogue

The traditional Aran fisherman's knitwear caught the eye of *Vogue* in 1955 when Digby Morton's stylish jumper dress, knitted in the Aran Islands in the iconic off-white wool, was featured in the September issue. From Marilyn Monroe and Grace Kelly to, more recently, Taylor Swift, the patterned sweater has received the superstar nod of approval on many occasions and is a wardrobe staple that surpasses trends. Frequently reinterpreted by designers, including Raf Simons and Simone Rocha, the iconic knit is still very much a classic and a lifelong investment.

48 Alexander McQueen
Tartan Dress

"I want to empower women. I want people to be afraid of the women I dress."
Alexander McQueen

This exquisitely tailored dress, made in the MacQueen wool tartan, was part of Alexander McQueen's Autumn/Winter 2006 collection "The Widows of Culloden", which explored his Scottish heritage. This one-shoulder dress, echoing the sash of traditional Highland attire, featured a figure-enhancing cinched-in waist, tulle skirt and broad leather belt. A version was worn by Sarah Jessica Parker to the "Anglomania" themed Met Gala. Although revered for his breathtaking and theatrical shows, McQueen was a master craftsman whose success lay in his unique fusion of innovation and tradition.

49
Sonja de Lennart
Capri Pants

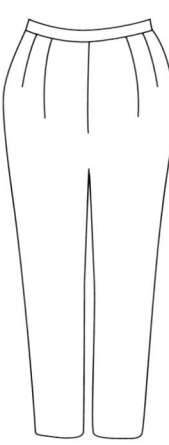

"Young people, who today can wear anything, do not know that this piece of clothing accompanied a social revolution."
Sonja de Lennart

Prussian-born fashion designer Sonja de Lennart is thought to have first introduced Capri pants in the mid 1940s, but Italian designers including Emilio Pucci are also often credited with the creation of this classic item. At a time when it was not commonly acceptable for women to wear trousers, de Lennart designed cropped, figure-hugging pants with side slits at the ankles to allow movement, as part of her "Capri" collection, named after her favourite island. The elegant style of trousers became synonymous with Hollywood chic after stars including Audrey Hepburn, Anita Ekberg and Elizabeth Taylor were pictured wearing them, and they endure as a wardrobe staple.

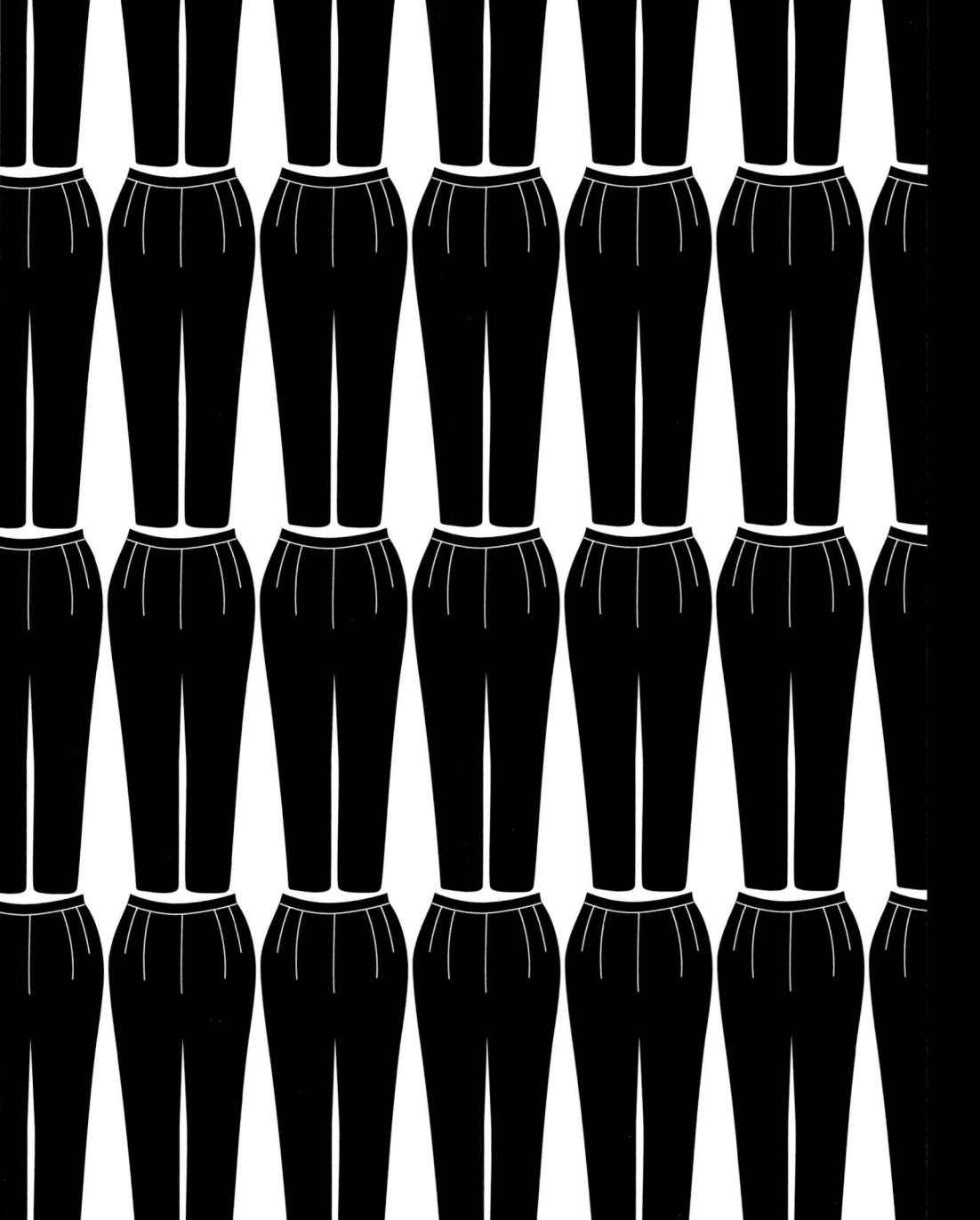

50

Gucci
Horsebit Loafer

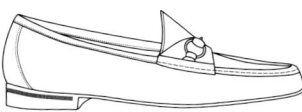

"Still one of the fashion pack's favourite shoes."
Harper's Bazaar

Aldo Gucci first designed the famous horsebit loafer in 1953 for men, inspired by the casual men's loafers he observed on visits to the US, but a version for women followed soon after. The Italian calfskin, simple silhouette and distinctive golden horsebit made them an instant classic, and the decades that followed saw them adopted among style-setters from Jane Birkin to Kendall Jenner. The Gucci loafer has endured for its craftsmanship, relaxed elegance and durability, and is one of the rare designs that never goes out of style.

51 Burberry Cashmere Scarf

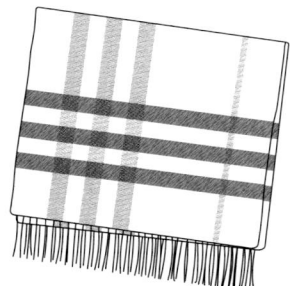

"Burberry is a British institution."
Naomi Campbell

From Anna Wintour to Alexa Chung and Sienna Miller, the distinctive Burberry scarf is a frequent favourite with the fashion pack. The Burberry check pattern first appeared in the 1920s as a rainwear lining. Woven on traditional looms, the cashmere scarf is made with impeccable craftsmanship and boasts more than 30 steps in its production. First introduced in the 1970s, the striking scarf with the classic Burberry check in camel, black, red and white is an investment piece that will last and transcend the latest trends.

52

Laulhère
Beret

"The most prestigious beret maker in France."
The New York Times

Maison Laulhère began making berets in 1840 and is the last historic manufacturer of the chic hats in France. Beret trends may come and go, but the simple felt hat remains a timeless wardrobe staple that can elevate the plainest of outfits and endures for its commendable practicality. From Brigitte Bardot and Joni Mitchell to Kate Moss and Beyoncé, the beret has been closely associated with a string of style icons and cultural groups through the decades, and is always guaranteed to make a statement, however you may choose to style it.

53 Louis Vuitton Speedy Bag

> **"Among the brand's many instantly recognizable styles, the Speedy is perhaps the most coveted."**
> *British Vogue*

One of the most famous bags in the world, the Louis Vuitton Speedy began life in 1930 as the "Express". Smaller than weekend bag the Keepall, the Speedy was designed for regular use, not just for travel. Made in cotton-canvas, it was light and practical, and originally available only in the 30-cm size. Audrey Hepburn requested a smaller version and, with her seal of approval, the Speedy 25 shot to stardom. Regularly spotted on A-listers from Dua Lipa to Miranda Kerr, the Speedy is known for collectible collaborations and innovative reiterations.

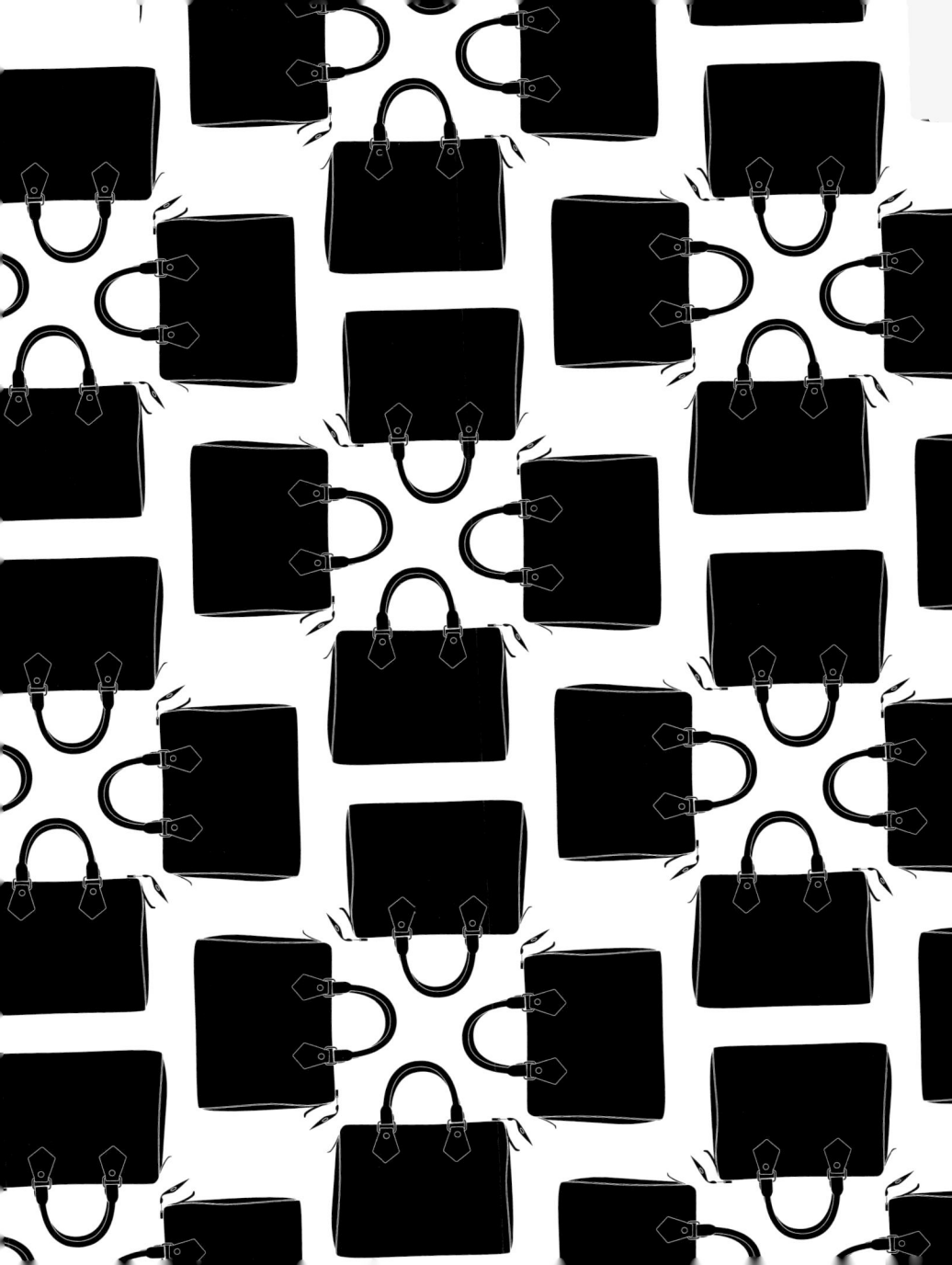

54

Chanel
Little Black Dress

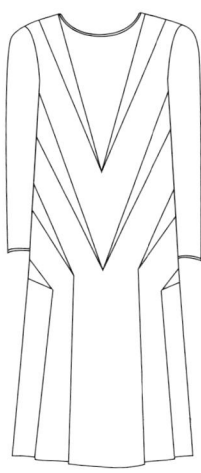

"The frock that all the world would wear."
Vogue

Coco Chanel is often credited with popularizing the little black dress with a design similar to this one that was illustrated in *Vogue* in 1926. Although modest black dresses were commonly worn by working-class women, and already becoming fashionable in high society, *Vogue* was perceptive in its predictions that Chanel's design would take the world by storm. This calf-length, long-sleeved silk dress captures an important moment in women's changing fashions. The "LBD" continued to make regular appearances in Chanel's collections and, despite changes of style through the years, the chic black frock remains a staple of women's wardrobes today.

55

Adidas
Tracksuit

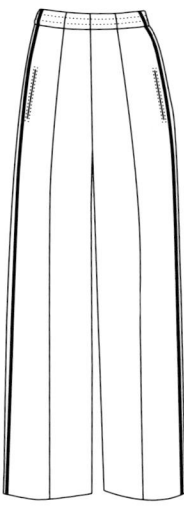

> "**I was mixing Adidas tracksuits and doing them in luxury fabrics... That, to me, was provocative.**"
> *Missy Elliott*

Adidas released its first sports tracksuit in 1967, specifically designed as a warm-up outfit, featuring the unmistakeable three stripes. During the 1970s the tracksuit became a popular leisurewear item and was adopted by subcultures including the burgeoning hip-hop scene. Missy Elliott wore a custom pink Adidas tracksuit to the Grammy Awards in 2003, and stars from Gracie Abrams to Rita Ora have embraced the iconic two-piece through the decades. The tracksuit trousers, in particular, have become a staple for everyone from the fashion pack to the A-list and, styling-wise, anything goes.

56 Fiorucci Stretch Jeans

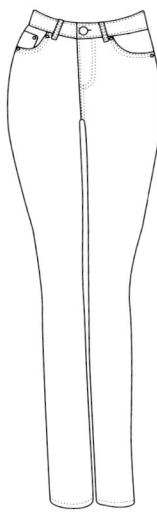

"Elio started making them tight, feminine… We brought jeans to America!"
Floria Fiorucci

Inspired by a visit to Ibiza in the 1970s, Italian designer Elio Fiorucci intuited that jeans should be cut to fit and flatter the bodies of women, leading to the design of his famous hip-hugging jeans. In 1982, he further innovated by adding Lycra to Fiorucci jeans to create the recognizable and enduring stretch silhouette. The global Fiorucci concept stores enjoyed cult status and reportedly attracted stars including Debbie Harry, Madonna, Andy Warhol and Cher. Skinny jeans certainly come and go in the fashion cycle, but you can guarantee a revival is always just around the corner.

57

Barbour Beaufort Waxed Jacket

"I love how timeless it is."
Alexa Chung

Originally inspired by traditional French shooting jackets, the Barbour Beaufort is the iconic garment that somehow became synonymous with royalty *and* Glastonbury. The signature Beaufort was first designed in 1983 by Margaret Barbour and the understated olive waxed cotton jacket has been through many iterations since. Appreciated for its exceptional quality, durability and functionality, the recognizable details such as the corduroy collar, practical pockets, tartan lining and relaxed fit make it a piece of classic design. Whether you choose to wear it with wellies or heels, the Beaufort is surprisingly versatile.

58 Chanel Slingback

"It's the most modern shoe and makes legs look beautiful."
Karl Lagerfeld

The iconic Chanel two-tone shoes with black tips were created in 1957 with shoemaker Raymond Massaro, and the successful collaboration continues to this day. Designed to flatter by lengthening the leg and making the foot look smaller, the legendary shoes had small heels and an elastic strap at the back, for comfort and practicality, and were originally beige and black. Karl Lagerfeld celebrated the style during his tenure at Chanel with multiple new interpretations including the popular ballet pump. Contemporary fans of the classic shoe include Brie Larson and Lily-Rose Depp.

59 Marc Jacobs
Stam Bag

> *"The transformation or the reinvention, I think, is the essence of what I've always loved about this."*
>
> *Marc Jacobs*

Maverick designer Marc Jacobs' iconic Stam bag debuted in 2005 and became a staple for the it-girls of the noughties. It was named after supermodel Jessica Stam and was beloved by everyone from Lindsay Lohan to Beyoncé. Its retro styling with an oversized fastening was unique and covetable. Although the design was retired in 2013, Jacobs revived the distinctive bag in 2023 in classic and little versions, and it looks set to remain a symbol for the label.

60

Jimmy Choo
Lance Sandal

"It is timeless and evolves each season."
Sandra Choi

The legendary Lance sandal debuted in 2008 and quickly became a frequent guest on the red carpet. The sandals' distinctive features included an open rounded toe, a pair of buckles at the ankle and the illusion of crossover straps at the front. The sophisticated evening shoe was seen on stars including Jennifer Aniston, Amal Clooney, Halle Berry and Charlize Theron. In recent years, the Lance evolved into the modern Azia.

61

Roland Mouret
Galaxy Dress

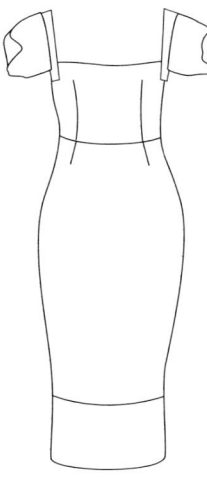

"You put it on and you looked like an icon."
Roland Mouret

First shown in 2005, Roland Mouret's curvy, figure-enhancing Galaxy dress became an instant but enduring bestseller and was worn by every A-lister going, from Sienna Miller to Cameron Diaz. According to Mouret, the secret of its success lay in the details of the construction, from the cinched-in waist to the supportive mesh inside, the elegantly folded sleeves, the perfectly positioned darts and the sensual square neckline. Beloved for its flattering silhouette, it is a lasting testament to the power of the dress.

62

Prada
Vela Backpack

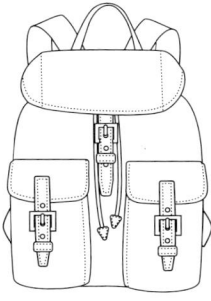

"I just wanted to search for the absolute opposite of what was already out there."
Miuccia Prada

In 1984, Miuccia Prada introduced the Vela backpack, a designer bag made with "Pocono" – a water-resistant durable nylon – which defied established ideas of luxury in the handbag market. The simple, strikingly chic backpack design reached a younger audience, and its popularity has endured for its distinctive covetable features and practicality. Prada invested years developing techniques to work with the unusual material and continues to innovate – the timeless design has since been relaunched using nylon made from discarded plastic.

63

Dior
Pencil Skirt

"A slim skirt must never be so straight that you cannot move in it."
Christian Dior

In 1954, Christian Dior's Autumn/Winter collection debuted the H-Line, with elegant suits featuring hip-emphasizing below-the-knee skirts that tapered at the bottom. Pencil skirts had previously been eclipsed by the full-skirted "New Look" and, although Dior was not alone in showing pencil skirts, the H-Line fast-tracked the new silhouette into the mainstream. At the time, the look, which lengthened the female form, was dubbed the "String Bean" by the press, and the skirt has remained a key element of many women's wardrobes through the decades.

64 Yves Saint Laurent
Safari Jacket

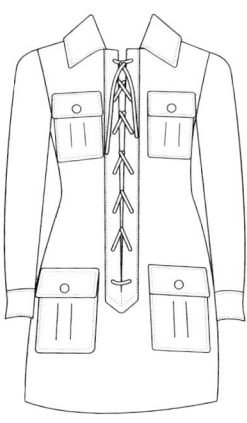

"This androgynous woman, on an equal footing with men through her clothes, upends the outdated image of classical femininity."
Yves Saint Laurent

In 1967, Yves Saint Laurent debuted a women's safari-inspired jacket, which was featured in *Vogue Paris* the following year. The distinguishing features of the safari jacket were the lightweight fabric, natural neutral colour, pockets and belted waist. Saint Laurent followed this with a version for his ready-to-wear "Rive Gauche" line in 1969. This "Saharienne" tunic was famously worn by Saint Laurent's muse Betty Catroux to the opening of his Rive Gauche store in London, and the distinctive new style for both men and women became widely fashionable.

65

Ray-Ban
Wayfarer Sunglasses

"I have a drawer full of them."
Debbie Harry

Modelled frequently by A-listers through the years, from Debbie Harry and Reese Witherspoon to Olivia Wilde and Emily Ratajkowski, Wayfarer sunglasses were first launched in 1952 and, with their sturdy plastic frames, are one of the most instantly recognizable fashion accessories. Designed by Raymond Stegeman for Ray-Ban, Wayfarers were catapulted to fame in the 1950s by Hollywood screen legends and have retained their cult status as a mid-century classic, rivalled only by Ray-Ban Aviator sunglasses for timeless style.

66

Yves Saint Laurent
Jumpsuit

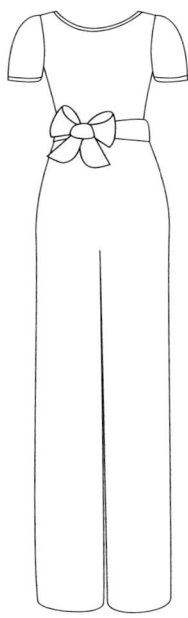

"My style is androgynous."
Yves Saint Laurent

Inspired by the practical attire of aviators, Saint Laurent presented his first jumpsuit in 1968. The elegant, short-sleeved one-piece with a defined waist was a stylish alternative to evening wear and reflected Saint Laurent's ambitions to give women confidence. Designers including Elsa Schiaparelli, Guy Laroche and Bonnie Cashin had previously experimented with the style, but Saint Laurent caused a stir, and it was seen as a bold fashion statement. The jumpsuit became wildly popular in the 1970s and continues to be a sophisticated choice today.

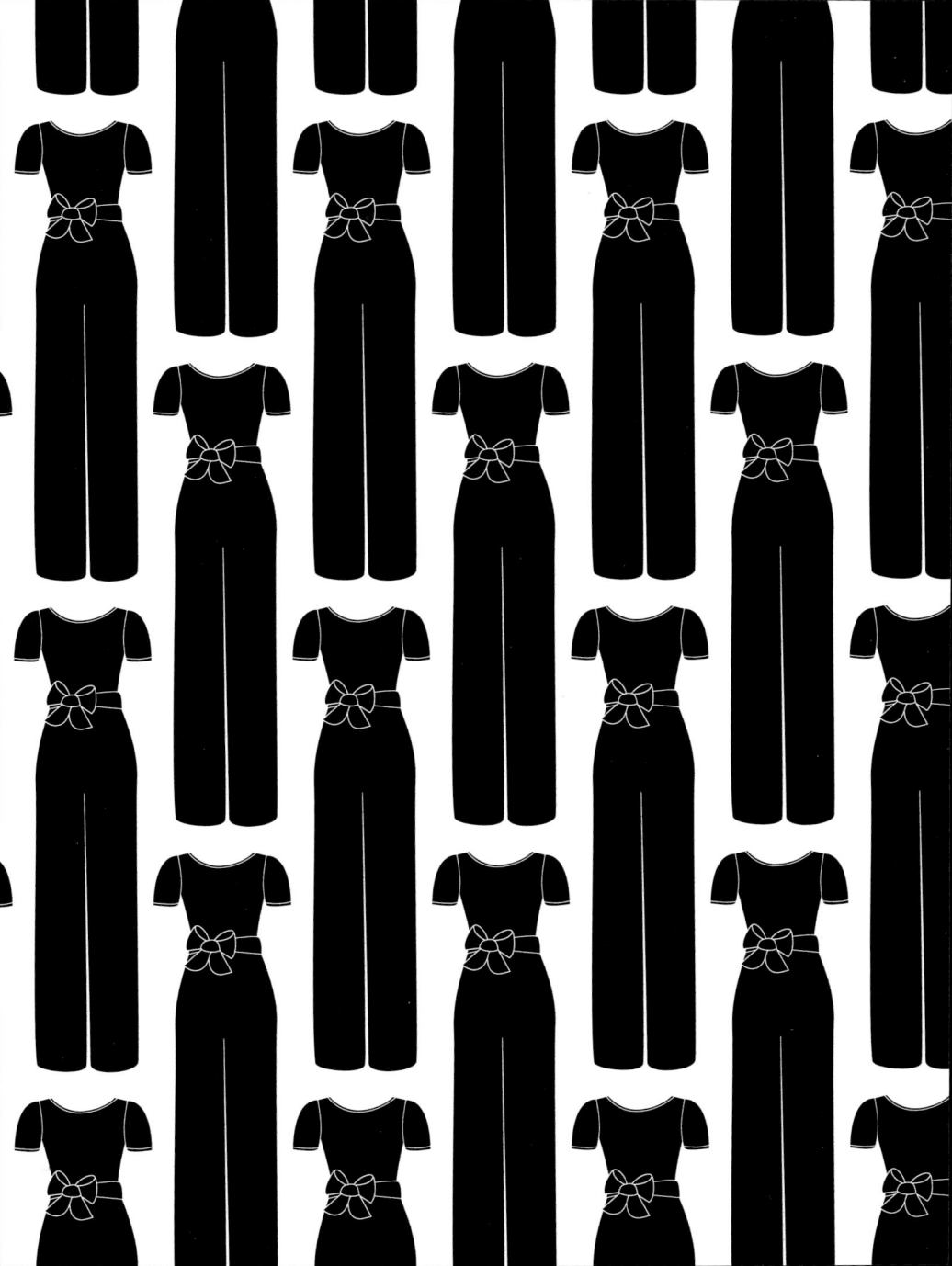

67

Givenchy Sheath Dress

> **"The little black dress is the hardest thing to realize, because you must keep it simple."**
> *Hubert de Givenchy*

Master couturier Hubert de Givenchy cemented the classic status of the little black dress forever with friend and muse Audrey Hepburn's iconic sheath dress in *Breakfast at Tiffany's*. The fitted satin dress with a nipped-in waist and unforgettable cut-out in the back, boldly revealing the shoulder blades, became synonymous with Hepburn chic and timeless style. Hepburn loved Givenchy designs for their "simplicity and beauty". The simple black sheath silhouette of 1961 has since been reinterpreted by Givenchy creative directors including John Galliano and Alexander McQueen.

68 Balenciaga Cocoon Coat

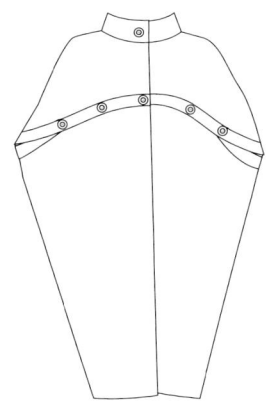

"Balenciaga alone is a couturier in the truest sense of the word."
Coco Chanel

As Cristóbal Balenciaga revealed his "Sack" dress in the late 1950s, he also presented new cocoon-like coat silhouettes. This woollen coat, tailored from one piece of fabric, freed the waist with a fluid but architectural shape. Balenciaga's experimental new designs were widely imitated and marked an important shift away from the waist-focused "New Look". Despite hiding a woman's figure, the cut was deemed flattering and elegant. Balenciaga's masterful tailoring made his innovative designs appear effortless.

69

New Era
59FIFTY Cap

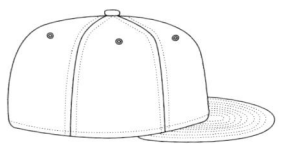

> "Back in the day it really wasn't a fashion thing, but now people wear the hats and it has nothing to do with sports."
> *Spike Lee*

New Era introduced the 59FIFTY baseball cap in 1954 and by the 1980s it was worn by players and fans alike. Previously available in team colours only, in 1996 film director Spike Lee requested a custom red Yankees cap, marking a new phase for the hat as it became available in customizable colours and reached a new audience. The iconic cap has become a shortcut to effortless style as this modern classic is worn the world over.

70

Chanel
2.55 Handbag

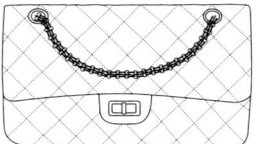

"Tired of carrying my bags by hand and losing them, I slipped a strap over them and slipped them over my shoulder."
Coco Chanel

In February 1955, Chanel created the iconic 2.55 handbag, based on an earlier creation from 1929, named after the month and year of its design. Made from soft quilted lambskin with a distinctive gold flat-link chain shoulder strap, the 2.55 allowed women greater freedom than the clutch or handled handbag, leaving hands free. The coveted features of the 2.55 include the "Mademoiselle" turn-lock closure and a secret pocket in the front flap. Chic owners through the decades include Jeanne Moreau, Jacqueline Kennedy and Jane Fonda.

71 Jacques Esterel
Bardot Top

> "**The Bardot phenomenon is an absolutely extraordinary phenomenon.**"
> *Jacques Esterel*

The sultry off-the-shoulder or slash-neck top highlighting the collar bone was popularized by iconic actress and model Brigitte Bardot in the early 1950s. Bardot wore a mix of haute couture and chic boutique finds, often wearing her own clothing in films. Designer Jacques Esterel created a black top with a "Bardot neckline" paired with a full gingham skirt for the starlet's performance in the 1959 film *Come Dance with Me!* He also designed the pink gingham wedding dress that caused a sensation at her nuptials the same year. From milkmaid tops to the boatneck, the influence of Bardot on fashion is still ubiquitous.

72

Jean Barthet
Wide-Brimmed Hat

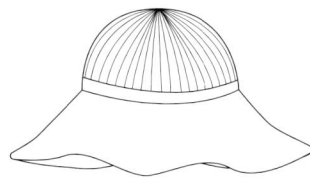

> "**Boasting more star-quality customers than any Hollywood studio ever had under contract.**"
> *Chicago Tribune*

Jean Barthet was a Parisian milliner who showed his first collection in 1949, and went on to cultivate an impressive client list including Brigitte Bardot, Grace Kelly and Sophia Loren. In a break from more formal hat silhouettes of the 1950s, Barthet – along with 1960s designers and style icons like Bardot – helped to make the oversized, floppy hat popular and associated with effortless chic. The wide-brimmed hat – whether straw, felt or linen – has continued to be a wearable fashion classic ever since.

73

Saint Laurent
Biker Jacket

"A wardrobe staple."
Harper's Bazaar

The classic biker jacket with zips we know today was designed and pioneered by Schott Bros co-founder Irving Schott in 1928. It became highly influential and nearly a century later endures as an iconic piece. Inspired by street styles, Yves Saint Laurent introduced a cropped leather jacket to a collection at Christian Dior in 1960, but it was not well received in high-fashion circles. Hedi Slimane's rock 'n' roll aesthetic during his tenure as creative director, from 2012–16, made the house the go-to for a timeless and authentically constructed piece. The appeal of the classic biker jacket lies in its durability and association with insouciant glamour.

74 Courrèges Go-Go Boot

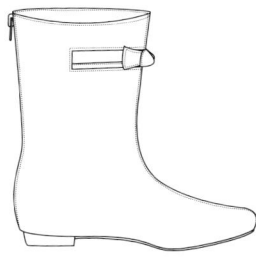

"You don't walk through life any more. You run. You dance."
André Courrèges

André Courrèges' highly influential "Space Age" collection of 1964 launched the minimalist flat boot into the stratosphere. The collection was inspired by space travel, and the designer's interest in futuristic technology was clear. The mid-calf, square-toed boots were comfy and allowed the wearer to move freely — and the simple style was copied around the world. These 1965 white boots include zips at the back and bold cut-outs at the front. The groundbreaking collection is still influential today and often referenced by contemporary designers.

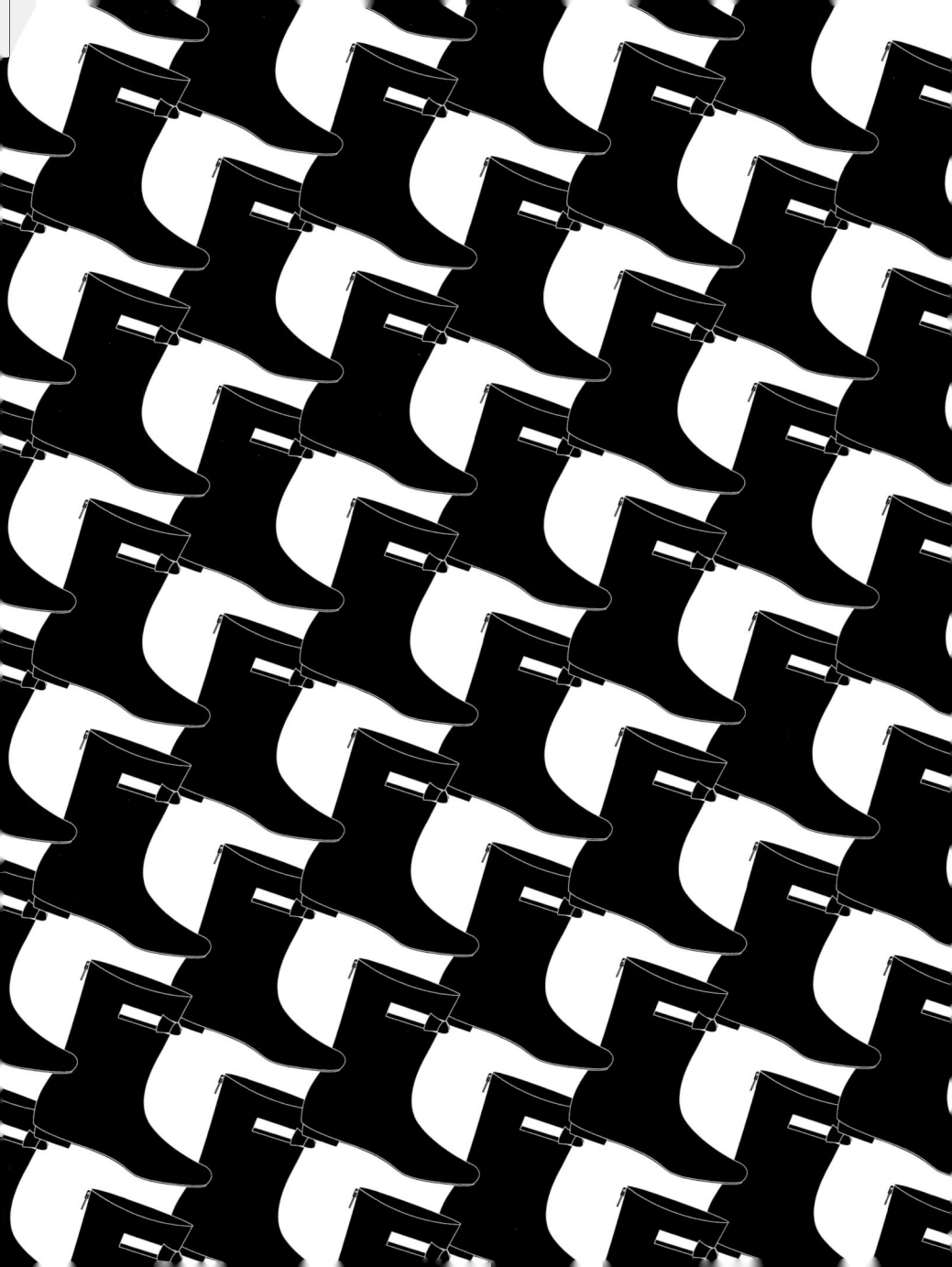

75

Claire McCardell for Townley Frocks
Popover Dress

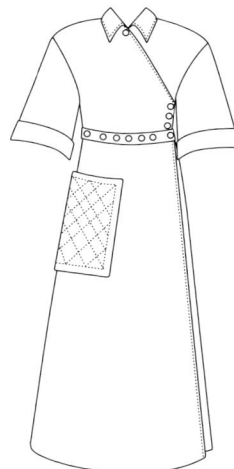

> *"Most of my ideas come from trying to solve my own problems – problems just like yours."*
> *Claire McCardell*

Claire McCardell designed mass-produced clothing for the modern housewife, and her "Popover" dress became wildly popular after its debut in *Harper's Bazaar* in 1942. The simple, hard-wearing, practical but elegant wrap-over design was made from durable cotton denim, and featured a large useful pocket and kimono-style loose sleeves for ease of movement. At once a cover-up, dress, coat and apron, it even came paired with a co-ordinated oven mitt! McCardell made stylish design accessible for every woman and the bestselling design has appeared in many different versions over the years.

76 Norman Norell
Mermaid Dress

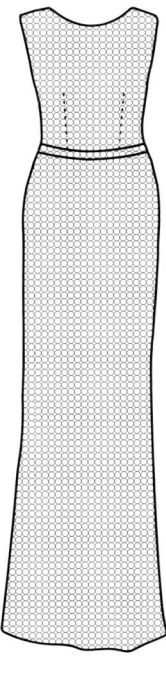

> "His marvellous cut and use of fabrics makes his things the most comfortable I've ever worn."
>
> *Lauren Bacall*

Often referred to as "America's Balenciaga" for his exemplary craftsmanship, designer Norman Norell created what came to be known as the "Mermaid" dress around 1952. Of the dress, he famously proclaimed, "In the evening, you have to knock 'em dead with glitter." The long, figure-hugging gowns were made with knitted silk jersey and shimmered with hand-stitched sequins. Lauren Bacall owned many of Norell's glittering dresses and Marilyn Monroe famously wore an emerald-green version to the Golden Globes in 1962. The simple round neck or V-neck were a signature of Norell's timeless but glamorous designs.

77 Adidas Samba Trainer

"Adidas Samba trainers have stood the test of time."
British Vogue

The famous Samba began its life in the 1950s when it was designed as a specialist football shoe, but the trainer we know and love today was launched in 1972. The classic shoe has been updated, refreshed and relaunched many times since, and modern collaborations have led to collectable editions. The unpretentious sneaker is a design classic and has global recognition. Regularly spotted on A-list fans, from Bella Hadid to Olivia Rodrigo, the staying power of the iconic Samba is incontrovertible.

78

Hermès
Kelly Bag

"A true fashion classic that will maintain its value."
British Vogue

Originally created in the 1930s by Robert Dumas, the Kelly bag was a reimagined Haut à Courroies – Hermès' first bag made to carry equestrian accessories. The beautifully crafted trapezoid bag shot to fame in the 1950s when Grace Kelly was photographed holding the bag to disguise her pregnancy and it was renamed the Kelly in her honour in 1977. The bag quickly became a coveted status symbol and, although notoriously difficult to acquire, the iconic Kelly remains a classic.

79 Vivienne Westwood Suit

> "I have taken the vocabulary of royalty and traditional British symbols – and used it to my advantage."
> *Vivienne Westwood*

The inventive tailoring and historical references in Vivienne Westwood's unique designs elevated the uninspiring suit to a work of art. This suit from the Harris Tweed collection of Autumn/Winter 1987 features her mini-crini skirt – a bell-like construction that became a signature Westwood look – and short double-breasted jacket. Tartan and Harris Tweed, a unique woven heritage fabric, were to become synonymous with Vivienne Westwood and her suits. From Helena Bonham Carter to Awkwafina, the A-list understands the power of a Westwood suit to make a style statement.

80 Jacques Fath
Cocktail Dress

"His clothes have ideas and flair. He makes you look young."
Harper's Bazaar

Couturier Jacques Fath's glamorous, waist-emphasizing silhouettes with full skirts and a playful lightness of touch were influential – along with Balmain and Dior – in determining the popular styles of the 1950s. Fath dressed stars including Rita Hayworth and Ava Gardner, and made Parisian style accessible to America with his line for manufacturer Joseph Halpert. This dress, made from black taffeta with distinctive large buttons and a voluminous skirt, demonstrates his skilful tailoring and gift for bold design. The classic 1950s silhouette is still as beautiful today as it was then and remains an elegant cocktail dress style.

81

Birkenstock
Arizona Sandal

"They have literally formed me physically and philosophically."
Frances McDormand

Launched in 1973, the unisex two-strap Arizona, designed by Karl Birkenstock, would become Birkenstock's bestselling model. Comfortable, practical but well-designed and stylish, the sandals proved to be a lasting classic. Widely loved and celebrated by everyone from celebrities and the fashion pack to ordinary folk, the distinctive sandals gradually found their way to iconic status after featuring in fashion shoots from the mid 1980s and into the 1990s. Frequent brand collaborations keep the sandals relevant and fresh, and they have become a wardrobe staple for many. Frances McDormand sealed their cult status by wearing custom Arizonas with her Valentino gown to the Oscars in 2019.

82

Hervé Léger
Bandage Dress

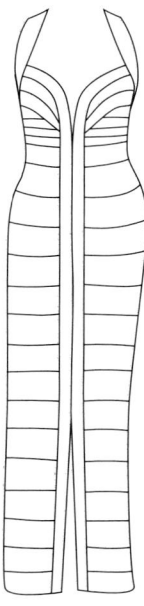

"The fit is great because it shapes the body."
Hervé Léger

In an era of innovative new bodycon dresses, including those by the "King of Cling" Azzedine Alaïa, Hervé Léger began experimenting with bands of metallic yarn moulded around the body to form a kind of modern corset. Léger debuted his bandage dresses on the catwalk in the early 1990s, worn by supermodels including Cindy Crawford and Naomi Campbell, but it was in the following decade that the figure-hugging dresses reached iconic status when they became beloved by celebrities including Victoria Beckham and Kim Kardashian. Flattering and empowering for a range of body types, the classic bandage dress is enjoying a revival.

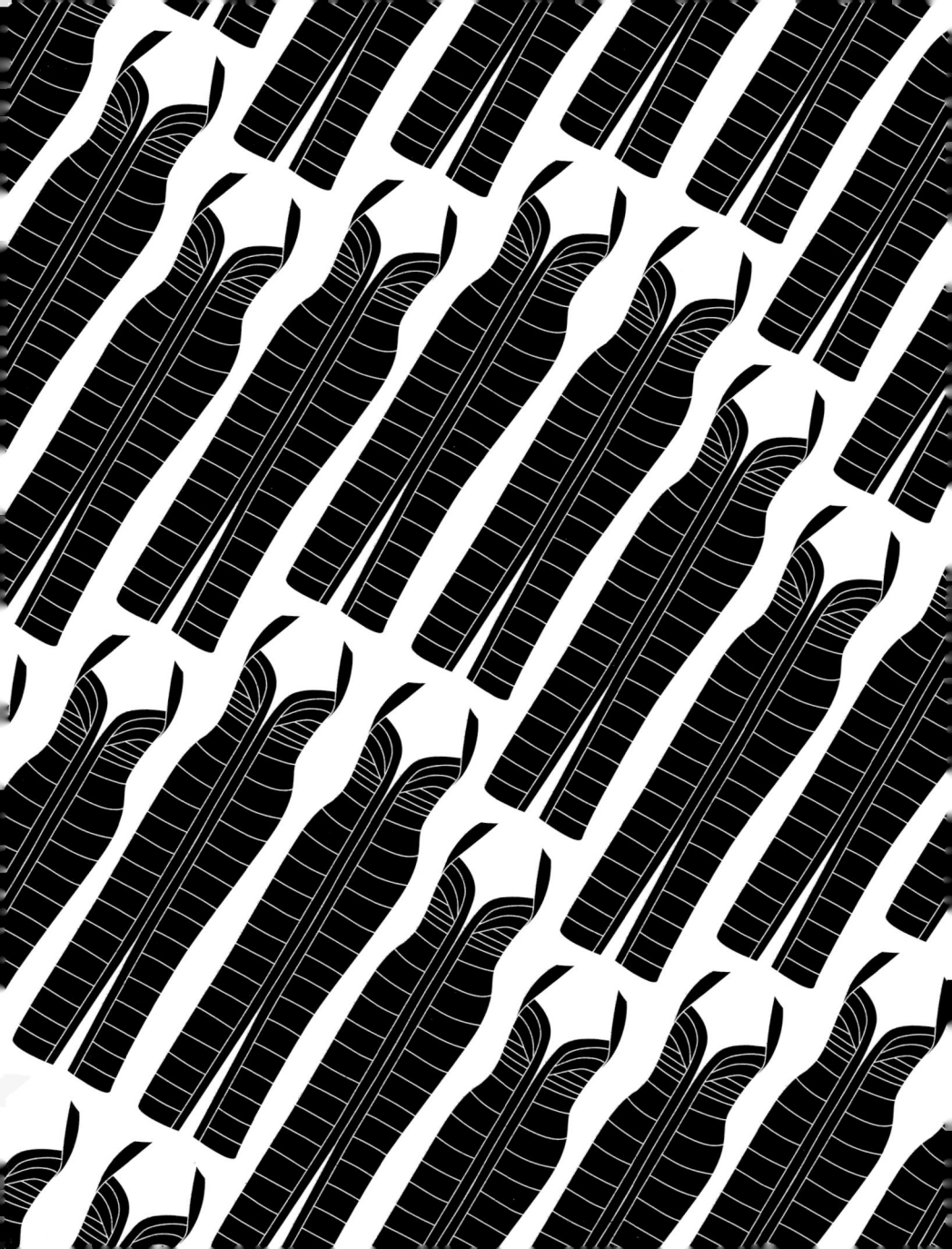

83

Alexander McQueen
Knuckle Clutch

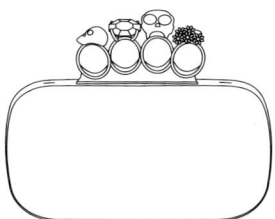

"You've got to know the rules to break them."
Alexander McQueen

The classic clutch is a useful and elegant piece in any wardrobe. Alexander McQueen was known for fusing death with beauty in his work and often used the skull as an aesthetic emblem. This iconic four-ring crystal-encrusted design featuring two skulls first appeared in 2009 and continues to evolve for the brand. Sought-after McQueen clutches are regulars on the red carpet and have been shown off by stars including Salma Hayek, Anne Hathaway and Emma Watson, and add a sophisticated edge to evening wear.

84

Dior
Aiguille Heel

"They finish the silhouette with a stroke of a pencil."
Roger Vivier

In 1954, Roger Vivier designed for Christian Dior an innovative "Aiguille" – or stiletto – with a steel pin inserted inside the wooden heel. This created a lighter and more practical stiletto for women, and the slender, elegant heels rapidly gained popularity during the decade. Christian Dior warned in his style guide *The Little Dictionary of Fashion*, published the same year, that heels "should never be too high, they look vulgar". Vivier, along with other innovative shoe designers including André Perugia and Salvatore Ferragamo – who famously designed a shoe with a 5-inch heel for Marilyn Monroe – changed the silhouette of women in the 1950s, and the stiletto has remained ubiquitous ever since.

85 Hermès Carré Scarf

"Every Hermès scarf has a tale."
Wall Street Journal

From the first design by Robert Dumas in 1937 to the more than two thousand that followed, the Hermès scarf is an accessory like no other. Desired for its sumptuous silk, craftsmanship and unique designs, the Carré – or square – scarf is an enduring and iconic accessory. From Madonna wearing the scarf as a top to Grace Kelly using one as a sling, the distinctive scarves have a history of unforgettable moments. Hermès keeps the magic alive with a continuous flow of artists creating new and sophisticated works of art.

86 Yohji Yamamoto
White Shirt

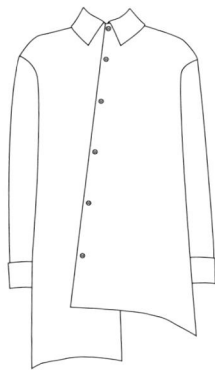

"You need the white shirt when you're wearing a black outfit to make it more challenging."
Yohji Yamamoto

Yohji Yamamoto's innovative white shirts are a powerful partner to the black suits for men and women he is renowned for. Often oversized, asymmetric or deconstructed and using unconventional textiles, the simple white shirt is elevated in the hands of the master tailor. Yamamoto's clothing frees women from traditional silhouettes, and his gender-neutral style is trend-surpassing and timeless. He said when he began designing for women, "All I wanted was for women to wear men's clothes."

87 Levi's Trucker Jacket

> **"The denim jacket belongs to American pop culture as much, if not more than, the blue jean."**
> *British Vogue*

Although Levi Strauss & Co. made its first denim jackets in the 1870s with the style evolving through the following decades, the classic Trucker, Lot No. 70505, was released in 1967. The iconic style caught on over the "Summer of Love" and the design was widely imitated all over the world. The denim jacket went through many iterations and innovations until this point and is still evolving today. The distinctive V-shaped diagonal seams, flap pockets and collar remain key signature details. Whether customized or battered, the Trucker is a wardrobe essential that is made to last.

88

Champion
Hoodie

"Hoodies are no longer for quiet nights at home."
Harper's Bazaar

The Champion "Reverse Weave" hoodie was first created in the 1930s as part of the brand's collegiate apparel range. The innovative fabric was designed to overcome shrinkage and the hoodie itself was developed as a pre-game garment and to keep sports players warm on the side lines. Hoodies became popular with university students in the following decades, but they exploded into mainstream culture with the rise of hip-hop in the 1980s. Champion remains a classic brand for hoodies, along with Nike and many others, and celebrity fans include Selena Gomez and Rihanna.

89

Manolo Blahnik
Maysale Mule

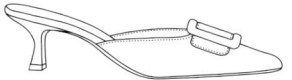

> **"Every five years or so, we revive it... It sells out every time."**
> *Manolo Blahnik*

Originally christened "Salem", the Maysale was first designed for Isaac Mizrahi's Spring/Summer 1991 collection and took inspiration from Pilgrim clothing. After Madonna was seen wearing the low heels at Cannes, Blahnik reported, "Suddenly everyone wanted a pair." The mules were soon widely adopted by the great and the good and have remained a lasting classic. With a distinctive buckle, kitten heel and a variety of finishes, the Maysale is a versatile shoe that adds an understated elegance to an outfit.

90 Dior Trapeze Dress

"The collection was absolutely beautiful."
The New York Times

In 1958, Yves Saint Laurent debuted his first collection for Christian Dior. He was the youngest couturier the world had seen, taking over the prestigious house at only 21 years old. His first collection was an overwhelming success and debuted the "Trapeze" line, a pioneering youthful shape that progressed Christian Dior's A-line collection of 1955. The simple but groundbreaking silhouette would become a defining style of the 1960s and has remained an influential shape through the decades.

91

UGG
Classic Mini Boot

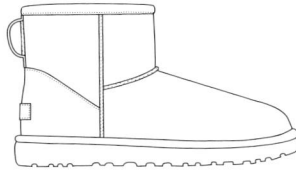

"A classic, something along the lines of a Barbour jacket."
Alexa Chung

It may divide opinion, but the fleecy UGG boot endures. The Californian brand, inspired by Australian surfer sheepskin shoes, took off in the 2000s when celebrities from Kate Hudson to Sienna Miller were frequently spotted wearing the casual footwear. UGGs are beloved for their supreme comfort, craftsmanship and durability. The classic ankle boot in chestnut looks set to stay, and there have been many popular unique collaborations with brands including Wales Bonner and Molly Goddard.

92

Dior
Turtleneck Sweater

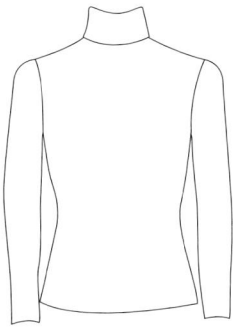

"Turtlenecks cushion, shield, and insulate a person from harm."
Diane Keaton

Yves Saint Laurent's provocative last collection for Dior in 1960 featured a black leather jacket and the all-important black turtleneck sweater. Saint Laurent's collection was inspired by the street style of beatniks, but the world of haute couture was not yet ready for the radical clothing. Although the style was ubiquitous among musicians and on the screen, designers such as Saint Laurent, Mary Quant and Halston helped to bring the turtleneck to the forefront of fashion in the 1960s and it remains a chic staple today.

93 Prada Galleria Handbag

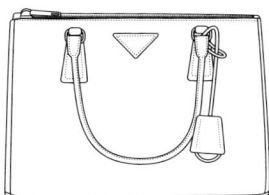

"With Mrs Prada, it's that thing of style with substance."
Marc Jacobs

Launched in 2007, the Galleria has become a symbol of Prada's identity and an example of the company's unmatched craftsmanship. The impeccably constructed bag is hand-finished and coveted for its heirloom qualities. The boxy shape echoes the traditional silhouettes of the past but with an added modern Prada twist. The distinctive Saffiano cross-hatched leather is scratch- and water-resistant and its features – such as a removable strap, sturdy handles and zipped pockets – make it a practical and durable option. The classic bag has been through many reinventions since its conception but retains its understated elegance.

94

Gianni Versace
Oroton Dress

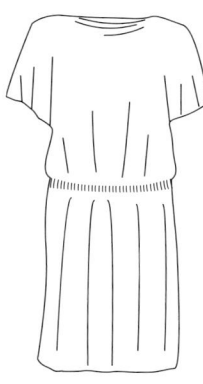

"I start with the textile... I like to invent something different."
Gianni Versace

Gianni Versace debuted this dress made from Oroton – an innovative lightweight fabric with a glittering, liquid metal effect – in 1982. Versace loved to experiment with materials and developed the groundbreaking textile with German atelier Friedrich Münch. The combination of this glamorous and light fabric that followed the figure, with the elegant and simple shapes of classical dress, made Versace's superfine chainmail dresses the "supermodel party look of choice" according to *Vogue*. It was fitting that Donatella Versace's 2018 show, honouring her brother's genius, ended with the supermodels Naomi Campbell, Claudia Schiffer, Helena Christensen and Carla Bruni adorned in shimmering gold Oroton dresses.

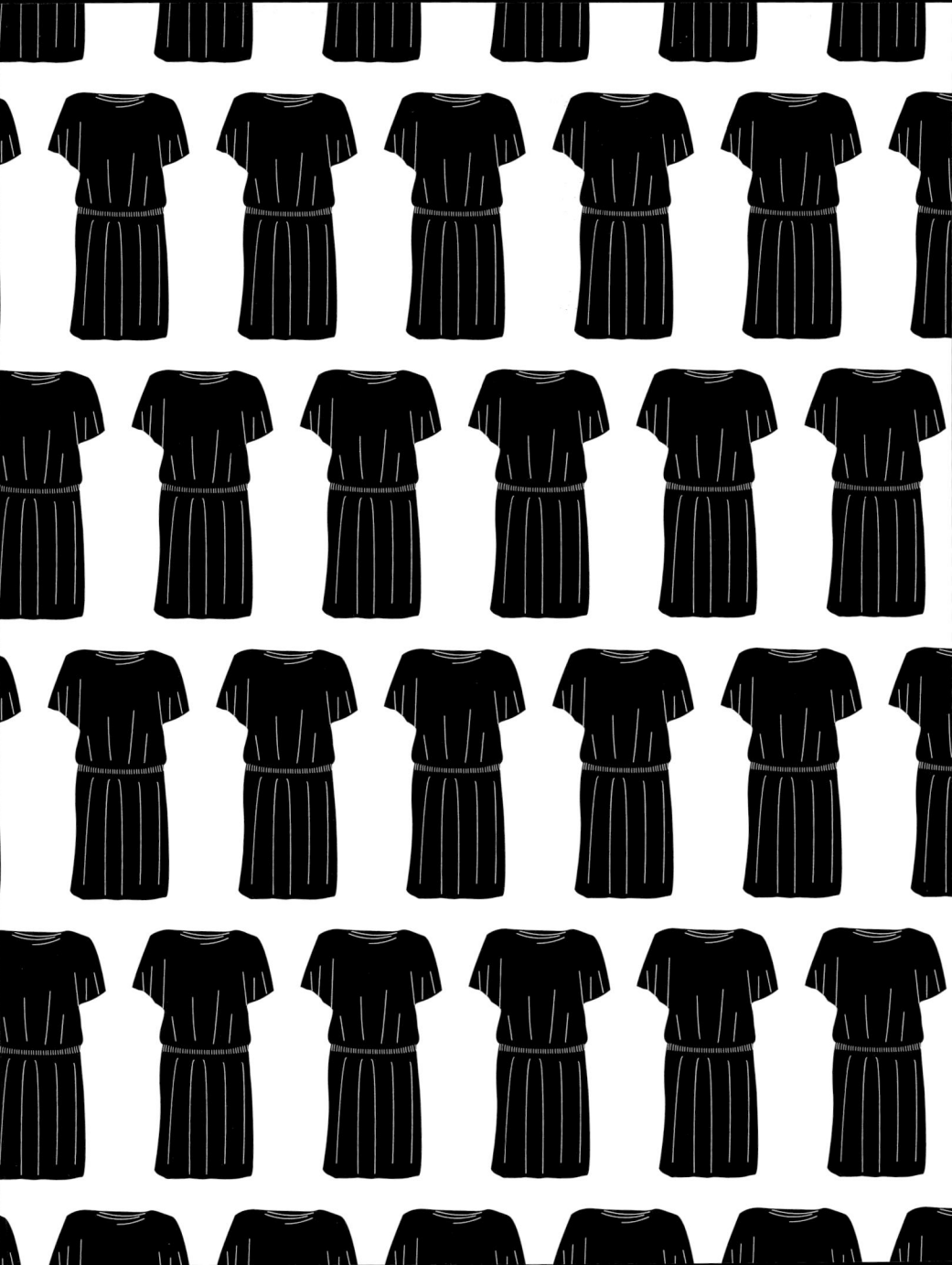

95

Alaïa
Zip Dress

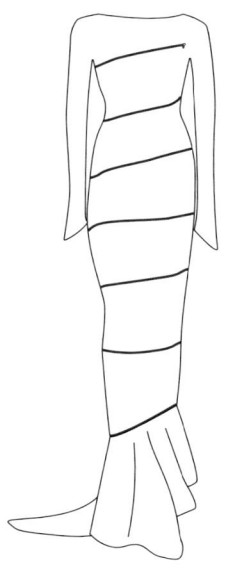

> "The first time I wore a piece of Alaïa, I had this sense of it being unlike anything I'd ever worn before."
>
> *Yasmin Le Bon*

Azzedine Alaïa was a firm favourite among fashion editors and stars alike for his innovative sculptural approach and pursuit of the ideal silhouette. Alaïa first created a spiralling zipped dress in 1981 – apparently inspired by French actress Arletty in the film *Hôtel du Nord* – and went on to design this long version in 2003. Zips were a frequent feature of Alaïa's revered designs and this skilfully cut dress – with a zip that wraps seven times around the body – is an iconic example of his mastery.

96

Lucchese
Cowboy Boot

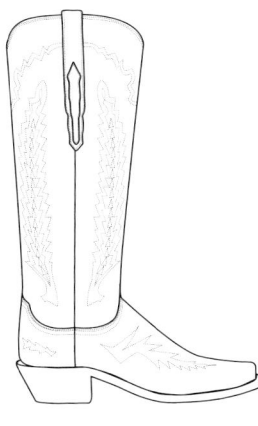

"This shoe brand is the go-to choice of icons."
Elle

Founded in 1883 by Salvatore Lucchese and brothers, the Texan brand's handmade boots are the ultimate luxury choice for Western footwear. The iconic cowboy boots have been seen on everyone from rock legends to movie stars, and they even received a name-check in the Beyoncé song "SWEET ★ HONEY ★ BUCKIIN'". Over the decades cowboy boots have remained a flattering and versatile choice, and the classic footwear has been championed by designers from Ralph Lauren and Calvin Klein to Isabel Marant and popularized by stars including Taylor Swift.

97
Gucci
Silk Shirt

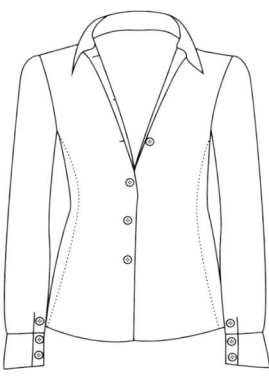

"It was so different than what we had been seeing in fashion."
Amber Valletta

Tom Ford's Autumn/Winter 1995 collection for Gucci catapulted him to fame and reinvigorated the Gucci brand. Amber Valletta and Kate Moss modelled unbuttoned tight jewel-toned silk shirts with figure-hugging velvet trousers and chunky belts, bringing sex back to the catwalk. Madonna wore the shirt shortly after at the MTV Awards and the glamorous look caught on around the world. The simple, 1970s-inspired design remains classic and immensely wearable today.

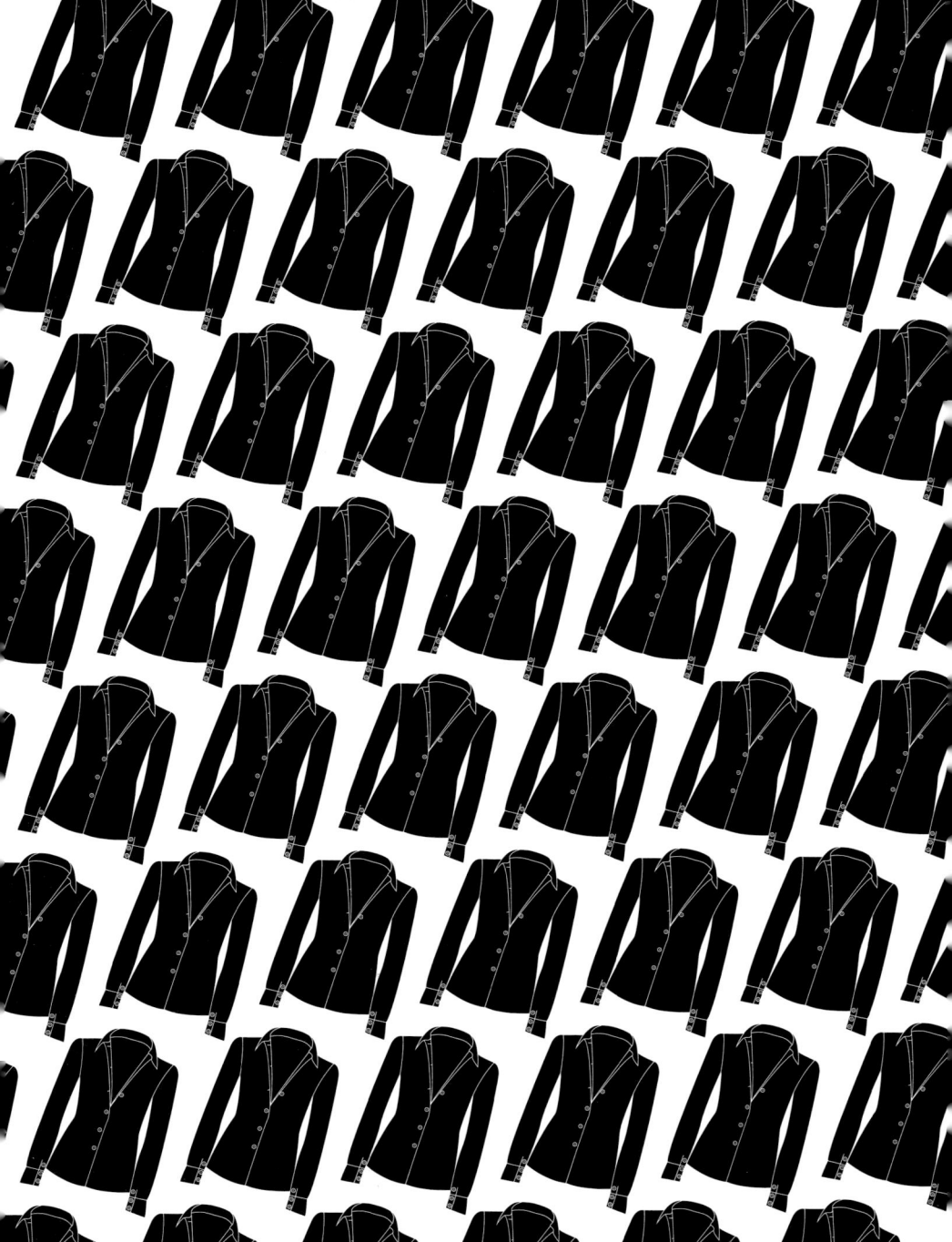

98

Valentino
Fiesta Dress

> **"For the Valentino maison, red is not just a colour. It is a non-fading mark, a logo, an iconic element of the brand, a value."**
> *Valentino Garavani*

Legendary Italian designer Valentino Garavani first included a red dress in his collection in 1959, and the red gown went on to become the signature of the house. The strapless "Fiesta" dress, embellished with tulle roses, encapsulated the designer's fascination with the deep-red shade "Rosso Valentino", which he considered a neutral colour. Valentino dressed many eminent people through the decades, from Audrey Hepburn to Jacqueline Kennedy, and the striking red dresses have been worn frequently on the red carpet – including by Jennifer Aniston, who sported the original 1959 design.

99

Hermès
Oran Sandal

> **"The Oran sandal was very special as it was not supposed to become a classic. It was just a simple flat, almost invisible."**
> *Pierre Hardy*

Created in 1997 by Hermès creative director Pierre Hardy, the relaxed Oran sandal with its distinctive H-shaped strap has become a must-have slider for fashion insiders and A-listers. The summer shoe was named after the city of Oran, Algeria, and was part of an African-inspired collection by Hardy. Minimalist and timeless, it's a comfortable and beautifully made sandal that has become a true classic. The bestselling shoe is continually revitalized in new colours and materials.

100 Salvatore Ferragamo Vara Ballet Flat

"When it was created, the boutique collection did not have a style that could be both casual and elegant."
Fiamma Ferragamo

Salvatore Ferragamo, shoemaker to the stars, famously custom-designed ballet flats for Audrey Hepburn in the style-setting film *Sabrina*. The classic Vara shoe was designed by Ferragamo's daughter, Fiamma Ferragamo, in 1978 and became an international bestseller, admired widely for the simple elegance of its design. The bow was originally intended to be leather but by a happy accident of miscommunication was made with the distinctive contrasting grosgrain ribbon that we know today. The Vara has evolved through many iterations, but the low heel, rounded toe and flat bow has remained a signature style for the company.

About the author

Clare Faulkner is an author, illustrator and graphic designer. She retrained in graphic design following a career in book publishing. During an inspiring 10 years at the V&A, she republished fashion gift books by Christian Dior, Hardy Amies and Edith Head, and launched a series of republished autobiographies by fashion designers including Paul Poiret, Barbara Hulanicki, Christian Dior and Elsa Schiaparelli. Clare has since worked on a diverse range of design projects, including books on fashion designers John Galliano and Victoria Beckham. She is also the author and illustrator of *The Cat Lover's A to Z* and *The Dog Lover's A to Z*, and illustrator of *The Little Book of Sloth Philosophy* and *Trash Animals*. She lives in London with her family.

Further reading

I would recommend the information-packed websites of the V&A (www.vam.ac.uk), The Met (www.metmuseum.org) and The Museum at FIT (www.fitnyc.edu/museum/), and the online archives of *Vogue*, *Elle* and *Harper's Bazaar*. Kerry Taylor Auctions also have a rich archive of fashion history to enjoy on their website (www.kerrytaylorauctions.com). These excellent books have been valuable resources in researching *The Fashion Classics: Fashion Evolution* by Paula Reed, *Fashion Designers A–Z* by Valerie Steele, *Items: Is Fashion Modern?* by Paola Antonelli and Michelle Millar Fisher, and *100 Ideas That Changed Fashion* by Harriet Worsley.

Acknowledgements

This book is dedicated to Mary Butler, the brilliant publisher at the V&A for many years, who was also a wonderful friend and mentor to everyone she worked with.

Thank you to Nicola Jöttkandt, for her help with the idea and scrutinizing the initial list, and to Frances Ambler, for her insightful read, but any errors or glaring omissions are entirely mine. Thank you too to all my other erstwhile colleagues at V&A Publishing for their support through the years.

I have been lucky to work with such a fabulous team at Summersdale, and in particular I would like to thank Claire Berrisford for commissioning the book and believing in my vision for it, Rebecca Haydon, Marianne Thompson, Debbie Chapman, Jasmin Burkitt and external editor Emily Kearns.

I am also grateful to my fantastic agent Euan Thorneycroft at A. M. Heath for his support and enthusiasm.

Finally, thank you to my eternally encouraging partner Ed and inspiring daughters, Edie and Rosa.

Have you enjoyed this book? If so, find us on Facebook at **Summersdale Publishers**, on Twitter/X at **@Summersdale** and on Instagram, TikTok and Bluesky at **@summersdalebooks** and get in touch. We'd love to hear from you!

www.summersdale.com